LOGOS

Season One

A spiritual voyage into the pages of the Bible

This page is intentionally left blank

LOGOS

Season One

A spiritual voyage into the pages of the Bible

by

Paul Banat & Richard Balfour

ISBN-13: 978-1-387-28713-0

First Printing

For information or to order additional books, please write:

The Next Generation Christians
61 16th Street
Roxboro, Quebec H8Y 1P1
CANADA

http://tngchristians.ca
tngchristians@gmail.com
1-800-847-7820

Table of Contents

A spiritual voyage into the pages of the Bible

Dedication

It is with great joy and thanksgiving that we dedicate this book to God the Father, Jesus Christ his only begotten Son, and the Holy Spirit. Without them, none of this would be possible.

We would also like to thank all the previous Biblical teachers, and pastors that we have learned from, and who have taught us many doctrines over the years, and we of course have kept the best, and now pass it on to you.

1Th 5:21 Prove all things; hold fast that which is good.

The list is too great to list here, but they know who they are, and also God knows who they are.

A spiritual voyage into the pages of the Bible

Use this space for notes

A few words from Paul

My voyage started many moons ago, but the year I got married was the year that I said to myself, enough is enough, it's time to learn the Truth.

I started reading the Book of Genesis and when I got to "and begat, and begat", I quickly changed my mind on how I was going to read the Bible. The next thing I bought was a KJV Bible Concordance, and started with searching the meaning of the original definition of words and all the places they appeared in the 66 authorized books of the King James Version.

That is how I got to see the "light" and see simple things like the difference between "Created" and "Made" and how God is very specific in choosing and using those two words; something many Rabbis, Pastors, and Biblical teachers have overlooked, and thus their teachings are questionable. They might sound Kosher, but that's all you get out of it, no definite proof of the truth.

I also never forgot what Jesus said!

> Joh_5:39   Search the scriptures; for in them ye think ye have eternal life: and they are they which testify of me.

The second thing I did was forget all that I had been taught and started from the beginning. I must have spent at least a few months just on the first two verses of the Bible.

Like most people in this world, I too was blind, but after praying for God to show me the Scriptures, He showed them to me in a new light, and I am going to try to teach you the truth as was intended from the beginning, hoping you join Richard and myself on this Spiritual voyage, that will definitely take us to stars in the near future.

> Ecc_12:12   And further, by these, my son, be admonished: of making many books there is no end; and much study is a weariness of the flesh.

So we will focus on the One Book, the Bible, for all our answers.

2Ti_2:15 Study to shew thyself approved unto God, a workman that needeth not to be ashamed, rightly dividing the word of truth.

Don't take our word!

1Th 5:21 Prove all things; hold fast that which is good.

A spiritual voyage into the pages of the Bible

Use this space for notes

A few words from Richard

From ever since I was a child, I was fascinated by the stars and the One who created them. Growing up in a Sabbath-keeping family, I heard every Bible story imaginable!

I always wondered what it would be like to live in Bible times. How amazing it would have been to witness miracles on a grand scale, and to live in an era when the Creator of the universe walked the streets of my neighborhood!

As I got older, the reality dawned on me that the society we live in hasn't changed that much from what we read in the pages of the Bible. I mean, sure we have neat inventions and electronic gadgets that weren't around back then, but socially we haven't matured or evolved much.

There's still a lot of hate, violence, and intolerance running rampant around the world. You'd think, that in the 2,000 years that have passed since the last acts of the Bible were penned, that the human condition would have improved somewhat. Unfortunately, this has not been the case!

Technology has done many great things, but it has not been able to bridge the gap and settle the differences between the different cultures, sexes, religions, and ways of life, and end the hate, hunger and suffering that have gone out of control in every "civilized" part of the world.

In the 1970's, the decade of my early childhood, a group of scientists launched a series of spacecraft into deep space, with the hopes that maybe one day in the distant future, they would have a chance encounter with an alien civilization.

It was hypothesized that IF these aliens could decode and follow the instructions inscribed on these discs, they would be able to see and hear the sights and sounds from planet Earth, and get a good description of the inhabitants that sent this "message in a bottle".

This message, frozen in time in the 1970s, will reach the closest star to our sun, Gliese 445, in about 45,000 years from now.

LOGOS represents our attempt to send a message, not to outer space, but right here, to all citizens of planet Earth. Our message, is the simple Truths revealed to mankind in the pages of the King James Version of the Bible.

This alien message is a message of hope for anyone that has questioned their life, especially after having lived through tough times or tragic losses.

Today, we are are a lost generation. Our kids are being dumbed down in schools, reputable news agencies are no longer trustworthy, weather patterns have changed significantly worldwide, our food chain is genetically modified, the cost of living has skyrocketed in recent years, traditional jobs have been replaced by computers and robots with artificial intelligence (A.I.), there are clashes between groups of almost every sort.

We have become slaves to greed and capitalism. Whether people realize it or not, **this is the cancer in our society**. It has spread to every part of the globe, thanks in part to the Internet, social media and smartphones.

We are already heavily dependant on silicon chips and mechanical devices for daily survival. If you don't believe me, just look at how the way we communicate with each other has changed with the introduction of the iPhone and devices similar to it.

The personal human touch has been replaced by screens and a myriad of emoticons! We check our phones for messages and redundant information more than we check what our Creator wants from us from day to day. Social media is the new opium of the masses, and it's not going away anytime soon!

Technology is essential to us in our day and age!

Many people can't imagine what their lives would be like without it. Should we wake up one day and they cease to work, all hell would break loose! Just cut a teenager's WiFi access for one day, or lose your phone somewhere and you'll see exactly what I mean!

The only technology required to read and understand the Bible, and the message within the pages and videos of our LOGOS project is to have an open mind that is willing to try new ideas, eyes to see and read without prejudice, ears to hear, hands to hold the pages and the time to sit and reflect on the words of these books, which we hope will help transform your life into what it was meant to be! No power outlet or batteries required (unless you're reading this in ebook format)!

We did our best to make the content of this book easy to understand, with no hidden messages or secrets, only the Truth as best as we could present it to you, with our limited reasoning and capacity to understand things as God sees them.

You've been given a free gift of a life free of pain and struggle, if you truly believe that Jesus Christ took your place on the cross and set you free, and WILL return one day soon to give you your reward for keeping the faith and believing his timeless message sent out to all citizens of planet Earth.

It doesn't matter how old you are, where you come from, what you did in the past, what gender you call yourself, or what your past or current religious beliefs and practices are if you're in jail or walking the streets freely.

We invite you to read the pages of the Bible, and we guarantee that you will see the Truth revealed to you in ways you never imagined possible before.

There is a new life waiting for you to discover, right here, right now! We hope you stay with us on this fantastic journey, as we prepare you for the next phase in our human evolution and history!

A spiritual voyage into the pages of the Bible

Use this space for notes

A Spiritual Voyage

Scan Me!

The Gospel of Christ dates back to Eternity past, even before the overthrow of the world.

> 1Pe 1:18 Forasmuch as ye know that ye were not redeemed with corruptible things, as silver and gold, from your vain conversation received by tradition from your fathers;

> 1Pe 1:19 But with the precious blood of Christ, as of a lamb without blemish and without spot:

> 1Pe 1:20 Who verily was foreordained before the foundation of the world, but was manifest in these last times for you,

> 1Pe 1:21 Who by him do believe in God, that raised him up from the dead, and gave him glory; that your faith and hope might be in God.

Accept this truth now, and if you don't, then once the Rapture takes place and you are left behind for the last seven years of this age, when the Angel preaches it, believe it, while you still have a chance!

> Rev_14:6 And I saw another angel fly in the midst of heaven, having the everlasting gospel to preach unto them that dwell on the earth, and to every nation, and kindred, and tongue, and people,

But why wait? You are here now, you can benefit right now, and guarantee your salvation today, for tomorrow might be too late!

The Old Testament saints were saved with the same faith in Christ, the only difference is that they looked forward to what Christ would accomplish on the cross, while today's saints look back at what Christ Jesus did on the cross.

> Gal_3:8   And the scripture, foreseeing that God would justify the heathen through faith, preached before the gospel unto Abraham, saying, In thee shall all nations be blessed.

A spiritual voyage into the pages of the Bible

Use this space for notes

Chapter 1
In The Beginning

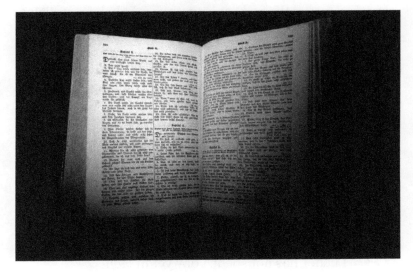

Gen 1:1 In the beginning God created the heaven and the earth.

What is stated above is all God has revealed at the beginning of the Bible concerning the origin of all things.

Lesson to learn from this is that God takes credit for all of creation, so if there was a Big Bang, then it was God who lit the fuse!

God did not spend too much time talking about the "World that then was" according to 2 Peter 3:5-7. The Bible was written for the present age of man, his fall, and his redemption to God, by God, thru God.

You might not have been taught this truth in school, or in churches, or on the web, this truth can only be revealed to you by God!

Our mission is to guide you on the right path to Biblical truths, and to make you into a Born Again Christian, for that is the sole purpose of the Bible.

Examples of a few false doctrines that have been around for years!

- Jesus was not born on December 25th.
- Jesus was not crucified on Friday.
- Noah did not spend 120 years building the Ark.
- Lucifer has not spent 1 day yet in Hell.
- There is no second chance.
- God did not create the world and everything in it in 6 days.
- The wise men were not present that night when Jesus was born.
- Jesus did not get a Christmas gift on His so called birthday of Dec, 25th.

If the above examples are new truths to you, then hold on for the rest of the revealed truths in the pages that follow.

Sagan or God

Scan Me!

No evolution taught in the Bible!

Carl Sagan was wrong!

The verses below are used to teach the creation of man and beasts on day 6. They are true statements; man and beast were created on the same day!

> Gen 1:24 And God said, Let the earth bring forth the living creature after his kind, cattle, and creeping thing, and beast of the earth after his kind: and it was so.

> Gen 1:25 And God made the beast of the earth after his kind, and cattle after their kind, and every thing that creepeth upon the earth after his kind: and God saw that *it was* good.

> Gen 1:26 And God said, Let us make man in our image, after our likeness: and let them have dominion over the fish of the sea, and over the fowl of the air, and over the cattle, and over all the earth, and over every creeping thing that creepeth upon the earth.

> Gen 1:27 So God created man in his *own* image, in the image of God created he him; male and female created he them.

The verses above give a quick recap of the events of day 6, yet the verses below give the order of creation of man and beasts on day 6!

So we have Adam butt naked being the first man created in God's image on earth.

> Gen 2:18   And the LORD God said, *It is* not good that the man should be alone; I will make him an help meet for him.

> Gen 2:19   And out of the ground the LORD God formed every beast of the field, and every fowl of the air; and brought *them* unto Adam to see what he would call them: and whatsoever Adam called every living creature, that *was* the name thereof.

> Gen 2:20   And Adam gave names to all cattle, and to the fowl of the air, and to every beast of the field; but for Adam there was not found an help meet for him.

So after Adam named all the beasts of the field and all the fowl of the air in the verses above, Adam had the first recorded plastic surgery. When he woke up, he was a rib short!

Personal note: This must be the reason I love spare ribs... missing that good old rib! Also of all the bones in my body, the only one I broke was a rib!

First Anesthesia and major operation recorded in the Bible!

> Gen 2:21 And the LORD God caused a deep sleep to fall upon Adam, and he slept: and he took one of his ribs, and closed up the flesh instead thereof;

Then God created the last creature of day 6, the Woman!

> Gen 2:22 And the rib, which the LORD God had taken from man, made he a woman, and brought her unto the man.

> *NOTE on the woman!* The word "Made" above is not the regular Hebrew word "ASAH" translated *made*, but BANAH, meaning the woman was *skillfully* formed. She was not made, she was built!

Then the last event to take place on day 6 was the first wedding recorded in the Bible! And like the naming of all built ships, Adam gave her a female name! He called her "WOMAN!" for she was *taken out* of man!

> Gen 2:23 And Adam said, This *is* now bone of my bones, and flesh of my flesh: she shall be called Woman, because she was taken out of Man.

> Gen 2:24 Therefore shall a man leave his father and his mother, and shall cleave unto his wife: and they shall be one flesh.

> Gen 2:25 And they were both naked, the man and his wife, and were not ashamed.

He only renamed her "EVE" after they *both* sinned, in the next chapter!

> Gen 3:20 And Adam called his wife's name Eve; because she was the mother of all living.

So, that leaves no time for evolution!

Evolution is nothing more that Devilution!

One more time!

God CREATED EVERYTHING!

A spiritual voyage into the pages of the Bible

Use this space for notes

Purpose of the Rapture

Scan Me!

There are no prophecies concerning the Rapture. It can happen anytime, thus triggering the next phase in God's plan.

To state it simply, there must be a Rapture of the true believers so that the Antichrist can come unto the scene!

The verses below do not teach about the Rapture, but the Second Advent. The message was intended for the Jewish people who do not believe in Jesus.

> Mat 24:33   So likewise ye, when ye shall see all these things, know that it is near, even at the doors.

> Mat 24:34   Verily I say unto you, This generation shall not pass, till all these things be fulfilled.

Everything listed in Mat. 24 will happen in **1 generation**, not many generations.

Now we know from Daniel and John that several things must take place BEFORE the Antichrist shows up.

- Babylon must exist as a city.

- There must be 10 kings in the old Roman Empire; then the Antichrist will rise from one of the future 10 kingdoms.
- The Jewish people will be sacrificing animals.

The Antichrist has nothing to do with the formation of the 10 kingdoms; He comes out of 1 of them, and conquers 3 of them. Egypt, Turkey and Greece, thus reviving the old Grecian empire.

Daniel mentioned 4 kingdoms. John mentioned 7 and then included an 8th.

What up with that?

> Rev 17:10 And there are seven kings: five are fallen, and one is, and the other is not yet come; and when he cometh, he must continue a short space.

> Rev 17:11 And the beast that was, and is not, even he is the eighth, and is of the seven, and goeth into perdition.

So who are the 5 fallen?

Answer:

1. Egyptian
2. Assyrian
3. Babylonian
4. Medo-Persian
5. Grecian

The "one is" in John's day was the Roman Empire.
The "other" is the revised Roman Empire, which will last 3 ½ years.

And the beast that was, "Grecian Empire" and was not in power in John's day is the eighth and is of the seven previous kingdoms that have oppressed Israel.

So,

1. Roman Empire

2. Revised Roman Empire with 10 rulers

3. Revived Grecian Empire with Antichrist as ruler of the 10.

   Rev 17:8 The beast that thou sawest was, and is not; and shall ascend out of the bottomless pit, and go into perdition: and they that dwell on the earth shall wonder, whose names were not written in the book of life from the foundation of the world, when they behold the beast that was, and is not, and yet is.

BONUS SECTION!

The bottomless pit is the Abyss, and only an angelic being could ascend from there! Giving his power to the Antichrist.

In case you do not know the different levels in Hell I will list them;

1. **Paradise**, which presently is closed and has two possible outcomes. First, it has been renovated to accommodate humans that go to hell. Second, it has become a museum for future generations to see how the old Testament saints lived after death before they were taken to Heaven.

2. **Tartarus**, which is a separate department for angels that had sexual relations with women.

3. **The Abyss**, "The bottomless pit" for demons and fallen angelic rulers.

4. **Hell**, "Sheol – Hades – Pit" the place of torment of all humans that have rebelled against God. This is where you will find Adam and Eve, not to mention Cain and all those that are not listed in Heb. 11.

5. **The Lake of Fire**, "The Gehenna of Fire" which is future will include all of the above departments except Paradise.

Here is what the residents of Hell have to say to the Antichrist!

> Isa 14:9 Hell from beneath is moved for thee to meet thee at thy coming: it stirreth up the dead for thee, even all the chief ones of the earth; it hath raised up from their thrones all the kings of the nations.

> Isa 14:10 All they shall speak and say unto thee, Art thou also become weak as we? art thou become like unto us?

> Isa 14:11 Thy pomp is brought down to the grave, and the noise of thy viols: the worm is spread under thee, and the worms cover thee.

First 2 individuals bodily cast into the Lake of Fire will be the Antichrist and his false prophet!

Rev 19:20 And the beast was taken, and with him the false prophet that wrought miracles before him, with which he deceived them that had received the mark of the beast, and them that worshipped his image. These both were cast alive into a lake of fire burning with brimstone.

Rev 20:10 And the devil that deceived them was cast into the lake of fire and brimstone, where the beast and the false prophet are, and shall be tormented day and night for ever and ever.

Hell will be stirred up! For the Antichrist, his final chance at stopping God's plan will have failed, and he will fail big time! Here is what the living nations have to say to the Antichrist!

Isa 14:16 They that see thee shall narrowly look upon thee, and consider thee, saying, Is this the man that made the earth to tremble, that did shake kingdoms;

Isa 14:17 That made the world as a wilderness, and destroyed the cities thereof; that opened not the house of his prisoners?

Isa 14:18 All the kings of the nations, even all of them, lie in glory, every one in his own house.

Isa 14:19 But thou art cast out of thy grave like an abominable branch, and as the raiment of those that are slain, thrust through with a sword, that go down to the stones of the pit; as a carcase trodden under feet.

Isa 14:20 Thou shalt not be joined with them in burial, because thou hast destroyed thy land, and slain thy people: the seed of evildoers shall never be renowned.

AMEN!

Qualifications for partakers in the upcoming Rapture.

The purpose of the upcoming Rapture is simple; to take out the living Christians on Earth before God unleashes His wrath on this rebellious planet.

If by chance you do not qualify for the first round of the Rapture, you will have a second chance during the two parts of the Tribulation period, but during that time **the final test will be dying in your faith for Christ!**

As far as present qualifications go one must "**Be Christ's**", "**Be in Christ**", "**Be in the Church**", and "**Be in the Body of Christ**."

There is only 1 way to qualify for that and that is to be **Born Again.**

To be "Born Again" follow the steps below:

1. Confess with the mouth that you are a sinner, and eternally lost.

2. Confess with the mouth that Jesus is the only begotten Son of God, who died in your place thus setting you FREE!

3. Believe in your heart that just as God raised Jesus from the dead to eternal glory, that you too will also be raised from the dead, not by your works, but by God's infinite grace.

4. Live by FAITH like Abraham, and most importantly die in FAITH, if the Rapture does not take place in your lifetime.

5. **(Optional)** Water Baptism is not essential for salvation, it simply is the believer's testimony of his/her belief that Jesus did die, that Jesus was buried, and that Jesus was BODILY resurrected 3 days later never to die again. Don't be intimidated by those "Water Baptizers" who insist you need to take a dip in the pool.

Then you will have done good, you will be blessed and holy. You will be in the way, the truth, and the life. You will be without spot or wrinkle and without blemish, you will be worthy.

If by chance you die before the Rapture, you will still be a partaker of the upcoming Rapture!

For all the dead since Christ's ascension will also be bodily resurrected and given glorified bodies at the same time as those still alive when it does finally take place.

1 Thes 4:16 For the Lord himself shall descend from heaven with a shout, with the voice of the archangel, and with the trump of God: and the dead in Christ shall rise first:

1 Thes 4:17 Then we which are alive and remain shall be caught up together with them in the clouds, to meet the Lord in the air: and so shall we ever be with the Lord.

1 Cor 15:51 Behold, I shew you a mystery; We shall not all sleep, but we shall all be changed,

1 Cor 15:52 In a moment, in the twinkling of an eye, at the last trump: for the trumpet shall sound, and the dead shall be raised incorruptible, and we shall be changed.

1 Thes 4:18 Wherefore comfort one another with these words.

We here at TNG Christians hope that you too will be part of this great resurrection of the dead in Christ.

So to end this lesson we will boldly declare that **as long as there is 1 Born Again Christian on the planet Earth, the Antichrist cannot come onto the scene**

A spiritual voyage into the pages of the Bible

Use this space for notes

Wings and Things

Scan Me!

There are 2 classes of fallen angels.

The first class are the ones now in Tartarus who committed a special sin.

> Gen 6:1 And it came to pass, when men began to multiply on the face of the earth, and daughters were born unto them,

> Gen 6:2 That the sons of God saw the daughters of men that they *were* fair; and they took them wives of all which they chose.

> Gen 6:3 And the LORD said, My spirit shall not always strive with man, for that he also *is* flesh: yet his days shall be an hundred and twenty years.

> Gen 6:4 There were giants in the earth in those days; and also after that, when the sons of God came in unto the daughters of men, and they bare *children* to them, the same *became* mighty men which *were* of old, men of renown.

> Gen 6:11 The earth also was corrupt before God, and the earth was filled with violence.

> Gen 6:12 And God looked upon the earth, and, behold, it was corrupt; for all flesh had corrupted his way upon the earth.

Gen 6:13 And God said unto Noah, The end of all flesh is come before me; for the earth is filled with violence through them; and, behold, I will destroy them with the earth.

Their goal was to corrupt the original makeup of man, creating half-breeds called Giants (verse 4).

There were 2 eruptions of these fallen angels among men, before and after Noah's flood!
(verse 4).

They broke God's law of reproduction of "After his/their kind".

<u>Note:</u> The giants have been judged and will not be judged again at the end of the Millennium.

Isa 26:14 *They are* dead, they shall not live; *they are* deceased, they shall not rise: therefore hast thou visited and destroyed them, and made all their memory to perish.

Back to the angels that sinned!

1Pe 3:19 By which also he went and preached unto the spirits in prison;

1Pe 3:20 Which sometime were disobedient, when once the longsuffering of God waited in the days of Noah, while the ark was a preparing, wherein few, that is, eight souls were saved by water.

2Pe 2:4 For if God spared not the angels that sinned, but cast *them* down to hell, and delivered *them* into chains of darkness, to be reserved unto judgment;

Jud 1:6 And the angels which kept not their first estate, but left their own habitation, he hath reserved in everlasting chains under darkness unto the judgment of the great day.

Jud 1:7 Even as Sodom and Gomorrha, and the cities about them in like manner, giving themselves over to fornication, and going after strange flesh, are set forth for an example, suffering the vengeance of eternal fire.

The second class are the ones still out there giving Lucifer a hand in trying to corrupt God's plan.

In total ⅓ of God's angels rebelled with Lucifer.

History of the World, Part Deux

Scan Me!

Let me start with this! Darwin was a fool!

> Gen 1:24 And God said, Let the earth bring forth the living creature <u>after</u> <u>his</u> <u>kind</u>, cattle, and creeping thing, and beast of the earth <u>after</u> <u>his</u> <u>kind</u>: and it was so.

> Gen. 1:25 And God made the beast of the earth <u>after</u> <u>his</u> <u>kind,</u> and cattle after their kind, and every thing that creepeth upon the earth <u>after</u> <u>his</u> <u>kind</u>: and God saw that *it was* good.

So much for evolution. God said the same thing for all plants, birds, and fish. I will not cut and paste but it's true. They will never find the "Missing Link" for it does not exist!

And if they still refuse to listen to sound Doctrine, let's look at;

> Gen. 2: 18 And the LORD God said, *It is* not good that the man should be alone; I will make him an help meet for him.

> Gen. 2:19 And out of the ground the LORD God formed every beast of the field, and every fowl of the air; and brought *them* unto Adam to see what he would call them: and whatsoever Adam called every living creature, that *was* the name thereof.

Gen. 2:20 And Adam gave names to all cattle, and to the fowl of the air, and to every beast of the field; but for Adam there was not found an help meet for him.

Gen. 2:21 And the LORD God caused a deep sleep to fall upon Adam, and he slept: and he took one of his ribs, and closed up the flesh instead thereof;

Gen. 2:22 And the rib, which the LORD God had taken from man, made he a woman, and brought her unto the man.

Notice how God slipped in verses 19-20 to show all living creatures were brought to him (Adam) in 1 day, not in billions of years. (Jesus, Jehovah at that time) and Adam in the great sandbox Doctrine!

Then the last creation of this present age was the woman.

So now you can answer the age old question: "What came first, the chicken or the egg?"

In case you doubt your answer it was the chicken!

The Pre-Adamites History

This history of Earth dates back from the first amoeba to the last dinosaur, science did get something right!

God created the Heavens first, then spirit beings and set-up principalities. Then He created the original Earth with Pre-Adamites all in the dateless past and never revealed to us how many moons had passed. Remember, this was all before Adam and Eve! (Gen. 1:1; Job 38:4-7).

God gave Lucifer rule over the Earthly kingdom (Rev. 12:12; Ezek. 28:11-18; Isa. 14:12-14).

After a long time, Lucifer sinned and invaded Heaven (He was not happy with what God gave him!) and he was defeated. As a consequence, his earthly kingdom was destroyed. (Gen. 1:2; Jer. 4:23-26; Ps. 104:5-9; 2 Pet. 3:5-6). In God's fierce anger and after God had totally destroyed all life on earth He then turned the earth upside down and flooded it, a process which caused the present formation of the Earth.

So there were 2 gardens of Eden on Earth. One in Lucifer's rule, the other in Adam's rule. I told you God destroyed Lucifer's Eden which was on a mountain and all gold and precious stones were scattered and buried along with all inhabitants and previous vegetation. Hence we dig for gold, precious stones, oil and gas!

Why else would God say this in Gen. 2:11?   The name of the first *is* Pison: that *is* it which compasseth the whole land of Havilah, where *there is* gold;

> Gen. 2:12 And the gold of that land *is* good: there *is* bdellium and the onyx stone.

The Heavenly City, presently located on the planet Heaven is full of gold and precious stones. That is where it all should have been here on earth too, but once again in God's fierce anger he destroyed it all. In Adam's garden there were no streets of gold and precious stones!

I look forward to the Heavenly City, for that is where all the saints will live for eternity.

Note: God will move that whole city to Earth after the Millennium, so Saints will not spend eternity in Heaven as taught by some!

You have read that Jesus went away to prepare a place ... and also, **in my Father's house are many mansions**, not tents, houses, condos but mansions. The rest of the surviving nations will live outside the Holy City, which is the New Jerusalem.

They will be able to visit, but never live there!

Strive now to get in!

It's a gated community with a 300 foot wall, and once the vacant spots are taken there will be no more new neighbours to welcome to the hood!

Rev. 21: 3 And I heard a great voice out of heaven saying, Behold, the tabernacle of God is with men, and he will dwell with them, and they shall be his people, and God himself shall be with them, and be their God.

Rev.21: 24 And the nations of them which are saved shall walk in the light of it: and the kings of the earth do bring their glory and honour into it.

Rev. 22: 2 In the midst of the street of it, and on either side of the river, was there the tree of life, which bare twelve manner of fruits, and yielded her fruit every month: and the leaves of the tree were for the healing of the nations.

Notice where the world's biggest oil reserves are!!!

That's right the Middle East, God has left his mark of a previous creation. God has always liked the Middle East.

In fact, He is moving The Holy City near to Jerusalem after the final cleanup of Sin!

The Eternal Plan from Eternity past to Eternity Future.

A brief history from eternity past to eternity future.

Below is God's plan from the beginning, to the end with His dealings with mankind. You might not get the "Big Picture" right now, but rest assured with the help of the Holy Spirit, you will fully understand the simple plan!

Here we go!

1. The Gods (Elohim) in the eternal past existed before anything in our known physical universe came into being. We are talking about before the "Big Bang!" There were and are 3 Gods, called **Elohim** in the *Old Testament*, and **Father**, **Son** and **Holy Spirit** in the *New Testament*.

2. The Gods then drafted the eternal plan of what They wanted to accomplish with "IF" "ELSE" statements. Meaning "IF" Lucifer never rebelled, then there was no need for Adam and Eve.

3. The Gods first created the heavens, our so-called universe. None of the Gods ever revealed how long it took them to accomplish this task.

4. They then populated the Heavens with innumerable angelic beings and created a home planet called Heaven.

5. Then the Gods created the Earth, with time populated it with intelligent carbon based beings and set Lucifer an angelic being as their ruler Gen.1:1, Isa. 45:18. (Way before Adam's day!) Remember the Gods love to share! All three are NOT SELFISH, the opposite most people I know down here on planet Earth.

6. Lucifer started the first rebellion in the universe against the Gods, and thus sin entered the universe long before the 6 days of Genesis.

7. The Gods put down the rebellion and destroyed all carbon-based life on earth due to sin. "The world that then was" according to Peter. This is recorded in Gen. 1:2, 2Pet. 3:5-7 and thus called Lucifer's flood.

8. Since the Gods created the Earth to be populated by carbon based beings, and not spirit beings, the Gods had to replace the previous inhabitants. Along came Adam and Eve, in the image of the Gods they were created and everything else you see in the present world today, in the 6 days of Genesis after Gen. 1:2.

9. The present ruler of Earth at this time was man.

10. Test of obedience to the Elohim's Word. Here comes that "if, then" statement again! Adam and Eve had to prove themselves to the Gods, for if an angelic being could sin, what about man? So the Gods gave man 5 commandments and the commandment of not to eat of the tree of knowledge of good and evil was broken.
Lucifer put doubt into Eve concerning what God plainly stated, and Eve even misquoted God's commandment and so she sinned, along with Adam.

This period is called the *dispensation of innocence.* This period did not last long, Lucifer did not waste time regaining dominion over this planet. According to my Jewish friends they estimate less than a week!

11. Now all mankind has sinned, for the whole human race was in Adam's "stones" but the Gods had prepared a plan even before mankind had sinned regarding a way to get mankind back into right standing with Them. This plan of course would not come to full completion for thousands of years. But was first promised in Gen. 3:15. It was a plan that involved all 3 members of the Godhead to accomplish.

12. Meanwhile mankind became so evil and corrupt that the Gods were about to wipe the whole human race out and start over again, The Gods had already done it once, so no big deal, but 1 man saved the world, Noah! This dispensation was called the *dispensation of conscience*, which lasted 1,656 years. It was from Adam to Noah's flood.

13. After the second flood recorded in Genesis, mankind did not take long to go back to the old ways, this is where all false religions come from, you can credit a Nimrod for that, and once again it came to the point where the Gods had to come down and confuse their language, and split them up. The earth was then split into continents in the days of Peleg. This dispensation was called *human government* and lasted 427 years. It was from after Noah's flood to the call of Abraham.

14. Then came the *dispensation of promise*, Abraham took centre stage. This dispensation lasted 430 years. From Abraham's call to the Exodus from Egypt.

15. Then came the *dispensation of the Law*. Moses was now the mediator between the children of Israel and the Gods. This Dispensation was from the giving of the Law to John the Baptist.

16. Then came the *dispensation of Grace*, Jesus now became the mediator of both Jews and Gentiles!

This dispensation has lasted so far over 1989 years and will end with the Rapture. Once it ends, then the last 7 years of the tribulation period before the next dispensation will take place. See The Book of Revelation Chapter 1:19 "things which must be hereafter" hereafter what? The churches!

> Rev. 1: 19 Write the things which thou hast seen, and the things which are, and the things which shall be **hereafter**;

After the Christians are Raptured!

17. Then will come the tribulation period, the last seven years before the Messiah (Christ) Jesus comes back. The Antichrist will only then be revealed by making a 7 year covenant with Israel. After he breaks it and seeks to destroy them, then Christ Jesus will come and fight for them (Children of Israel) at Armageddon. **Note:** The US is not involved here!

18. After this dispensation will come the *dispensation of Divine Government*, which will last 1,000 years. Mankind will be ruled by Jesus and all the redeemed from Abel's time.

19. At the end of that dispensation, Lucifer will be released for a short season of 3 ½ years to test those that lived thru the tribulation. One last battle between good and evil will take place. All rebels

will be put down by God the Father this time. We will then enter the last dispensation, the *Dispensation of the Redeemed and faithful Angels* this Dispensation will go on for all eternity.

20. God will renew the Heavens and the Earth, like He did in the 6 days of Genesis, then God will transfer His Holy City, The New Jerusalem to this now final SINLESS world and thus dwell among MEN for all eternity.

The Key to Revelation

Scan Me!

The Book of Revelation is not a hard book to understand, for the definition of *revelation* is the act of revealing or disclosing, or making something obvious and clearly understood.

So why do so many people make it a mystery?

Because they do not take the time to get to know God! Simple as that! They prefer to listen to some Preacher who may or may not know what he is talking about, but has a mega church full of The Walking Dead!

The book can be divided into 4 sections, and then the 4th section can be subdivided for easier understanding.
The Book of Revelation is in "Chronological order" no jumping back and forth in it!

Hope you learn something here, and clearly see that until the end of the church age, anything written in the book of Revelation after chapter 4 **cannot happen until the "Rapture" has taken place!**

Important note: The rapture can happen at anytime. There are no signs given to when it might happen, **so you have to be ready every day!** This might also help to explain why some (but not all) true Christians might seem obsessed about talking to others about this amazing, once-in-a-lifetime opportunity!

At that point, God will start dealing with the Jews again. The rest of the book you can say deals mainly with the Jews and God's wrath on sinners.

My new saying is: "That when Paul is gone, then shall the end start!"

For after the "Church Age, or Dispensation of Grace" ends, God will once again deal with the Jews again. He has not dealt with them since they crucified Jesus back in 30 A.D.

> Mic_5:3 Therefore will he give them up, until the time that she which travaileth hath brought forth: then the remnant of his brethren shall return unto the children of Israel

Now let's start dividing!

Section 1: Rev. 1:1-11

Introduction to the book of Revelation.

Section 2: Rev. 1:12-20

The things which thou hast seen...

The vision of Christ...

Section 3: Rev. 2:1 – 3:22

The things which are...

The churches.

Section 4: Rev. 4:1 – 22:5

The things which shall be hereafter...

After the churches.

6 Subsections

1. Rev. 4:1 – 5:14 - Vision in Heaven.

2. Rev. 6:1 – 18:24 - Daniel's 70th week fulfilled.

3. Rev. 19:1 – 20:3 - Second Advent (coming) of Jesus. Battle of Armageddon. Satan is bound for 1000 years. The "Millennium." Starts.

4. Rev. 20:4 – 20:15 - After 1000 years Satan is released for a "little season" about 3 1/2 years to deceive the nations. Final destruction of Satan and all evil beings. Judgement of all sinners all of them sent to the lake of fire bodily for eternity.

5. Rev. 21:1 – 22.5 - New Heavens and Earth. Note. The oceans will be gone, meaning more parking space!

6. Rev. 22:6 – 20 - Conclusion.

Key to the Book of Revelation

The Book of Revelation is like any other book, just read it as a normal book and you will see that there is nothing mystical about it.

The problem is that too many false teachers have put out so much false teachings and confused even Confucius!

The book is in chronological order in its message; there is no jumping back and forth in it.

Now below is the key to understanding the book, it is all summed up in 1 verse, see verse below!

> Rev 1:19 Write the things which thou hast seen, and the things which are, and the things which shall be hereafter;

So there you go, was that hard to understand?

It is divided by the "things" for you in 3 parts and each part cannot start until the previous part has been completed!

1. The things which thou hast seen

The vision of Christ in the midst of the candlesticks
Rev. 1

COMPLETED

2. The things which are

The churches Rev. 2-3

(PRESENTLY IN THIS PART. WILL BE
COMPLETED ONCE THE RAPTURE TAKES
PLACE.)

3. The things which shall be hereafter

After the Rapture of the Church Rev. 4-22

Daniel's 70th week, the last 7 years of the times of
the Gentiles starts and ends.

**This part will only start AFTER the Rapture; No
prophecy in it shall take place while the Church
(Body of Christ) is still on Earth!**

A spiritual voyage into the pages of the Bible

Which Came First?

Scan Me!

Abraham was a Christian!

God never gave old Abe the Law!

> Gal_3:8   And the scripture, foreseeing that God would justify the heathen through faith, preached before the gospel unto Abraham, *saying,* In thee shall all nations be blessed.

So if you do not understand the Scripture verse above let me explain it to you!

The Bible consists of 2 Testaments, the Old Testament and the New Testament.

What the verse above is teaching is that Abraham followed the New Testament teachings!

God gave the Children of Israel the Old Testament which was NOT the one He gave Abraham!

> Deu 5:2   The LORD our God made a covenant (The Old covenant) with us in Horeb.

> Deu 5:3   The LORD made not this covenant (The Old Covenant) with our fathers (Abraham, Isaac, Jacob), but with us, *even* us, who *are* all of us here alive this day.

The days are coming when once again the Jews will accept the New Covenant!

Jer 31:31 Behold, the days come, saith the LORD, that I will make a new covenant with the house of Israel, and with the house of Judah:

Jer 31:32 Not according to the covenant (The Old Covenant) that I made with their fathers (in Moses' days) in the day *that* I took them by the hand to bring them out of the land of Egypt; which my covenant they brake, although I was an husband unto them, saith the LORD:

Jer 31:33 But this *shall be* the covenant (The New Covenant) that I will make with the house of Israel; After those days, saith the LORD, I will put my law in their inward parts, and write it in their hearts; and will be their God, and they shall be my people.

Jer 31:34 And they shall teach no more every man his neighbour, and every man his brother, saying, Know the LORD: for they shall all know me, from the least of them unto the greatest of them, saith the LORD: for I will forgive their iniquity, and I will remember their sin no more.

So stick with the New Covenant and live by Faith in Jesus Christ like Abraham did!

Gal 3:7 Know ye therefore that they which are of faith, the same are the children of Abraham.

Use this space for notes

Chapter 2
The Mission Jesus Came To Do

Christ's mission was simple and twofold!

The first part:

REDEEM man was what God commanded Christ Jesus to do.

Do it at all cost was the decree.

He came, and accomplished His work.

A spiritual voyage into the pages of the Bible

The second part:
So called the Second Advent.

His mission will be to:

- destroy all those that have not accepted God's free gift
- setup the Millennial Kingdom of Heaven and properly evangelize the world

You are presently living in between His two missions, Jesus is in Heaven seated on the right side of God the Father.

If you have not yet accepted God's free gift of eternal life in Jesus, then I suggest you do it now, for when Christ gets off His throne you will not want to be here for His Second Advent. So **#TakeAKnee** NOW!

If you have accepted Christ Jesus, then you too will come back with Christ on His Second Advent.

Passover or Easter?

Scan Me!

WARNING! BIBLICAL TRUTH REVEALED!

Jesus was crucified on Wednesday!

Joh 20:1 The first day of the week cometh Mary Magdalene early, when it was yet dark, unto the sepulchre, and seeth the stone taken away from the sepulchre.　Early, when it was yet dark, Before it became light on Sunday morning, which day began at sunset Saturday and ended with sunset Sunday.

Gen 1:5 And God called the light Day, and the darkness he called Night. And the evening and the morning were the first day.

So we know that the first day mentioned is Sunday which starts Saturday night to Sunday night.　Jesus our Lamb of God was killed on the 14th of Nisan.

Exo 12:6 And ye shall keep it up until the fourteenth day of the same month: and the whole assembly of the congregation of Israel shall kill it in the evening.

Jesus died at 3:00 PM Wednesday (day) on the 14th of Nisan which on our Gregorian calendar fell on Wed the 3rd of April in 30 A.D, or in the Hebrew year of 3790.

Note: The Gregorian year of 2017 is the equivalent of 5777, which means that the Crucifixion took place 1987 years ago.

He remained DEAD for 3 full days and 3 full nights a full 72 hours!

Wednesday (night) ☾

Thursday (day) ☼

1 st day

Thursday (night) ☾

Friday (day) ☼

2 nd day

Friday (night) ☾

Saturday (day) ☼

3 rd day

Jesus rose soon after sunset Saturday night which then became (Early) Sunday the first day! (This is according to how God counts starting and ending times for days).

> Joh 20:17 **Jesus saith unto her,** Touch me not; for I am not yet ascended to my Father: but go to my brethren, and say unto them, I ascend unto my Father, and your Father; and to my God, and your God.

Jesus ascended to Heaven and came back the same day! Now that's FAST, faster than the speed of light! Jesus told her this Saturday night (Early Sunday).

> Joh 20:19 Then the same day at evening, being the first day of the week, when the doors were shut where the disciples were assembled for fear of the Jews, came Jesus and stood in the midst, and saith unto them, Peace be unto you.

Now this was still Sunday before the sun set completely. So you see, Mary saw him Saturday night, and now it was Sunday evening when Jesus came back.

> Joh 20:26 And after eight days again his disciples were within, and Thomas with them: then came Jesus, the doors being shut, and stood in the midst, and said, Peace be unto you.

The next Sunday! Notice that the Early Christians gathered on Sundays, and not on the Sabbath like the Jews! Pentecost fell on Sunday that year also, and they were baptized in the Holy Spirit also on a Sunday!

> Lev 23:5 In the fourteenth day of the first month at even is the LORD'S passover.

> Lev 23:6 And on the fifteenth day of the same month is the feast of unleavened bread unto the LORD: seven days ye must eat unleavened bread.

> Lev 23:7 In the first day ye shall have an holy convocation: ye shall do no servile work therein.

> Lev 23:8 But ye shall offer an offering made by fire unto the LORD seven days: in the seventh day is an holy convocation: ye shall do no servile work therein.

So 14th of Nisan is the Lord's Passover not a high Sabbath. On the 15th of Nisan is the feast of unleavened bread, the first day and the seventh day are high Sabbaths.

> Mat 12:40 For as Jonas was three days and three nights in the whale's belly; so shall the Son of man be three days and three nights in the heart of the earth.

> Deu 21:22 And if a man have committed a sin worthy of death, and he be to be put to death, and thou hang him on a tree:

> Deu 21:23 His body shall not remain all night upon the tree, but thou shalt in any wise bury him that day; (for he that is hanged is accursed of God;) that thy land be not defiled, which the LORD thy God giveth thee for an inheritance.

Reason for breaking legs? The high Sabbath was going to start in 4 hours.

> Mat 27:62 Now the next day, that followed the day of the preparation, the chief priests and Pharisees came together unto Pilate,

> Mat 27:63 Saying, Sir, we remember that that deceiver said, while he was yet alive, After three days I will rise again.

Mat 27:64 Command therefore that the sepulchre be made sure until the third day, lest his disciples come by night, and steal him away, and say unto the people, He is risen from the dead: so the last error shall be worse than the first.

Mat 27:65 Pilate said unto them, Ye have a watch: go your way, make it as sure as ye can.

Mat 27:66 So they went, and made the sepulchre sure, sealing the stone, and setting a watch.

This was Wednesday sunset to Thursday sunset. This was the high Sabbath, not the regular weekly sabbath.

Luk 24:1 Now upon the first day of the week, very early in the morning, they came unto the sepulchre, bringing the spices which they had prepared, and certain others with them.

This is anytime after sunset Saturday which then is our Sunday! Remember Jesus was the lamb that was slain, and that was on the 14th of Nisan outside the city walls.

On yet another Passover/Feast of unleavened bread.

Act 12:3 And because he saw it pleased the Jews, he proceeded further to take Peter also. (Then were the days of unleavened bread.)

Act 12:4 And when he had apprehended him, he put him in prison, and delivered him to four quaternions of soldiers to keep him; intending after Easter to bring him forth to the people.

This is the only time in the whole Bible that the word *"Easter"* is used. It should have been translated *"Passover"* like the other 28 times in the New Testament!

G3957
πάσχα
pascha
Total KJV Occurrences: 29

passover, 28

Mat_26:2, Mat_26:17-19 (3), Mar_14:1, Mar_14:12 (2), Mar_14:14, Mar_14:16, Luk_2:41, Luk_22:1, Luk_22:7-8 (2), Luk_22:11, Luk_22:13, Luk_22:15, Joh_2:13, Joh_2:23, Joh_6:4, Joh_11:55 (2), Joh_13:1 (2), Joh_18:28, Joh_18:39, Joh_19:14, 1Co_5:7, Heb_11:28

easter, 1

Act_12:4

Even if you persist on it being Kosher, remember this took place in Israel and the date was the Jewish date of the month of Nisan 14 - 21, which this year started on April 10th in the evening and ended in the evening of April 18 2017.

Celebrating afterwards is nice, but you missed the Biblical truth!

A spiritual voyage into the pages of the Bible

Use this space for notes

Aleph Tav & Alpha Omega

Scan Me!

Rev_22:13 I am Alpha and Omega, the beginning and the end, the first and the last.

Joh_5:39 Search the scriptures; for in them ye think ye have eternal life: and they are they which testify of me.

Joh 1:1 In the beginning was the Word, and the Word was with God, and the Word was God.

Joh_1:2 The same was in the beginning with God.

Joh_1:3 All things were made by him; and without him was not any thing made that was made.

Joh 1:4 In him was life; and the life was the light of men.

Joh 1:5 And the light shineth in darkness; and the darkness comprehended it not.

Let's look at the beginning! Those numbers are called Strong's numbers and give the original definition of the word.

Gen 1:1 In the beginning[H7225] God[H430] created[H1254 (H853)] the heaven[H8064] and the earth.[H776]

Now if you pay attention there is ONE WORD NOT SHOWN in the English Translation!

(H853) את

In the original Hebrew text, the Aleph (א) Tav (ת)! In Greek, Alpha (α) and Omega (Ω)!

Let's look at the 6 days of Genesis and find out who God was talking to!

Day 1 Aleph Tav "(H853)" divided light from darkness;

> Gen 1:3　　And God[H430] said,[H559] Let there be[H1961] light:[H216] and there was[H1961] light.[H216]

> Gen 1:4　　And God[H430] saw[H7200] (H853)the light,[H216] that[H3588] *it was* good:[H2896] and God[H430] divided[H914] [H996] the light[H216] from[H996] the darkness.[H2822]

Day 2 Aleph Tav made the Firmament and divided the waters;

> Gen 1:6　　And God[H430] said,[H559] Let there be[H1961] a firmament[H7549] in the midst[H8432] of the waters,[H4325] and let[H1961] it divide[H914] [H996] the waters[H4325] from the waters.[H4325]

Gen   1:7   And   God[H430]   made[H6213]   (H853)   the firmament,[H7549] and divided[H914] [H996] the waters[H4325] which[H834]*were* under[H4480] [H8478] the firmament[H7549] from[H996] the waters[H4325] which[H834]*were* above[H4480] [H5921] the firmament:[H7549] and it was[H1961] so.[H3651]

Day 3 Aleph Tav did not do anything on this day, God commanded the waters and the Earth to do the work! (Remember Aleph Tav created the Earth in verse 1!)

Gen   1:9   And   God[H430]   said,[H559] Let the waters[H4325] under[H4480]   [H8478]   the heaven[H8064] be gathered together[H6960] unto[H413] one[H259] place,[H4725] and let the dry[H3004]*land* appear:[H7200] and it was[H1961] so.[H3651]

Gen   1:10   And   God[H430]   called[H7121] the dry[H3004]*land* Earth;[H776] and the gathering together[H4723] of the waters[H4325] called[H7121] he Seas:[H3220] and God[H430] saw[H7200] that[H3588]*it was* good.[H2896]

Gen   1:11   And God[H430] said,[H559] Let the earth[H776] bring forth[H1876]   grass,[H1877]   the herb[H6212] yielding[H2232] seed,[H2233]*and* the fruit[H6529] tree[H6086] yielding[H6213] fruit[H6529] after his kind,[H4327] whose[H834] seed[H2233]*is* in itself, upon[H5921] the earth:[H776] and it was[H1961] so.[H3651]

A spiritual voyage into the pages of the Bible

Gen 1:12   And the earth[H776] brought forth[H3318] grass,[H1877]*and* herb[H6212] yielding[H2232] seed[H2233] after his kind,[H4327] and the tree[H6086] yielding[H6213] fruit,[H6529] whose[H834] seed[H2233]*was* in itself, after his kind:[H4327] and God[H430] saw[H7200] that[H3588]*it was* good.[H2896]

Day 4 Aleph Tav set up the solar system's time clock

Gen 1:14   And God[H430] said,[H559] Let there be[H1961] lights[H3974] in the firmament[H7549] of the heaven[H8064] to divide[H914] [H996] the day[H3117] from[H996] the night;[H3915] and let them be[H1961] for signs,[H226] and for seasons,[H4150] and for days,[H3117] and years:[H8141]

Gen 1:15   And let them be[H1961] for lights[H3974] in the firmament[H7549] of the heaven[H8064] to give light[H215] upon[H5921] the earth:[H776] and it was[H1961] so.[H3651]

Gen 1:16   And God[H430] made[H6213] **(H853)** two[H8147] great[H1419] lights;[H3974] **(H853)** the greater[H1419] light[H3974] to rule[H4475] the day,[H3117] and the lesser[H6996] light[H3974] to rule[H4475] the night:[H3915]*he made* the stars[H3556] also.

A spiritual voyage into the pages of the Bible

Day 5 Aleph Tav created all sea creatures great and small and all birds in the firmament.

Gen 1:20   And God[H430] said,[H559] Let the waters[H4325] bring forth abundantly[H8317] the moving creature[H8318] that hath life,[H5315] [H2416] and fowl[H5775]*that* may fly[H5774] above[H5921] the earth[H776] in[H5921] the open[H6440] firmament[H7549] of heaven.[H8064]

Gen 1:21   And God[H430] created[H1254] **(H853)** great[H1419] whales,[H8577] and every[H3605] living[H2416] creature[H5315] that moveth,[H7430] which[H834] the waters[H4325] brought forth abundantly,[H8317] after their kind,[H4327] and every[H3605] winged[H3671] fowl[H5775] after his kind:[H4327] and God[H430] saw[H7200] that[H3588]*it was* good.[H2896]

Day 6 Aleph Tav created all land animals and man.

Gen 1:24 And God[H430] said,[H559] Let the earth[H776] bring forth[H3318] the living[H2416] creature[H5315] after his kind,[H4327] cattle,[H929] and creeping thing,[H7431] and beast[H2416] of the earth[H776] after his kind:[H4327] and it was[H1961] so.[H3651]

Gen 1:25 And God[H430] made[H6213] **(H853)** the beast[H2416] of the earth[H776] after his kind,[H4327] and cattle[H929] after their kind,[H4327] and every thing[H3605] that creepeth[H7431] upon the earth[H127] after his kind:[H4327] and God[H430] saw[H7200] that[H3588]*it was* good.[H2896]

Gen 1:26   And God[H430] said,[H559] Let us make[H6213] man[H120] in our image,[H6754] after our likeness:[H1823] and let them have dominion[H7287] over the fish[H1710] of the sea,[H3220] and over the fowl[H5775] of the air,[H8064] and over the cattle,[H929] and over all[H3605] the earth,[H776] and over every[H3605] creeping thing[H7431] that creepeth[H7430] upon[H5921] the earth.[H776]

Gen 1:27   So God[H430] created[H1254] (H853)man[H120] in his *own* image,[H6754] in the image[H6754] of God[H430] created[H1254] he him; male[H2145] and female[H5347] created[H1254] he them.

I will end with the following question!

Zec_12:10 And I will pour upon the house of David, and upon the inhabitants of Jerusalem, the spirit of grace and of supplications: and they shall look upon **me whom they have pierced**, and they shall mourn for him, as one mourneth for *his* only *son*, and shall be in bitterness for him, as one that is in bitterness for *his* firstborn.

Who is the *"Me whom they have pierced?"*

Answer!

and they shall look[H5027] upon[H413] me(H853) whom[H834] they have pierced,[H1856]

There are over 7,000 Aleph Tav's placed in the Old Testament, you just have to search the scriptures like Jesus the Aleph Tav said!

The Old Testament is packed with over   7,000 aleph tav's which credit the second person of the Trinity as the God "Eloah" (אלוה) responsible.

Gen 1:1 In the beginning God created the heaven and the earth

Gen 1:1 בְּרֵאשִׁית[H7225] בָּרָא[H1254] אֱלֹהִים[H430] אֵת[H853] הַשָּׁמַיִם[H8064] וְאֵת[H853] הָאָרֶץ:[H776]

Notice both places above with H853

H853

את
'êth

Gen 1:4 And God saw the light, that *it was* good: and God divided the light from the darkness.

Gen 1:4 וַיַּרְא[H7200] אֱלֹהִים[H430] אֵת[H853] הָאוֹר[H216] כִּי[H3588] טוֹב[H2896] וַיַּבְדֵּל[H914] אֱלֹהִים[H430] בֵּין[H996] הָאוֹר[H216] וּבֵין[H996] הַחֹשֶׁךְ:[H2822]

Gen 1:16 And God made two great lights; the greater light to rule the day, and the lesser light to rule the night: *he made* the stars also.

Gen 1:16 [H6213]וַיַּעַשׂ [H430]אלהים [H853]אֵת [H8147]שְׁנֵי [H3974]המארת [H1419]הגדלים [H853]אֵת [H3974]המאור [H1419]הגדל [H4475]לממשלת [H3117]היום [H853]ואת [H3974]המאור

A spiritual voyage into the pages of the Bible

Use this space for notes

A Tale of Two Kingdoms

Scan Me!

The Bible not only teaches the 1st and 2nd coming of Christ to the earth but also the 1st and 2nd coming of God the Father to the Earth.

The first coming of God the Father will be at Armageddon to help Christ defeat and destroy the Antichrist's kingdom and give the kingdom over to Christ and the saints.

> Dan 7:9 I beheld till the thrones were cast down, and the Ancient of days did sit, whose garment *was* white as snow, and the hair of his head like the pure wool: his throne *was like* the fiery flame, *and* his wheels *as* burning fire.

> Dan 7:13 I saw in the night visions, and, behold, *one* like the Son of man came with the clouds of heaven, and came to the Ancient of days, and they brought him near before him.

> Dan 7:14 And there was given him dominion, and glory, and a kingdom, that all people, nations, and languages, should serve him: his dominion *is* an everlasting dominion, which shall not pass away, and his kingdom *that* which shall not be destroyed.

> Dan 7:22 Until the Ancient of days came, and judgment was given to the saints of the most High; and the time came that the saints possessed the kingdom.

Zec 14:5   And ye shall flee *to* the valley of the mountains; for the valley of the mountains shall reach unto Azal: yea, ye shall flee, like as ye fled from before the earthquake in the days of Uzziah king of Judah: and the LORD my God shall come, *and* all the saints with thee.

Tit 2:13   Looking for that blessed hope, and the glorious appearing of the great God and our Saviour Jesus Christ;

The second coming to earth will be at the end of the Millennium.

1Co 15:24   Then *cometh* the end, when he shall have delivered up the kingdom to God, even the Father; when he shall have put down all rule and all authority and power.

1Co 15:25   For he must reign, till he hath put all enemies under his feet.

1Co 15:26   The last enemy *that* shall be destroyed *is* death.

1Co 15:27   For he hath put all things under his feet. But when he saith all things are put under *him, it is* manifest that he is excepted, which did put all things under him.

1Co 15:28 And when all things shall be subdued unto him, then shall the Son also himself be subject unto him that put all things under him, that God may be all in all.

Eph 1:10 That in the dispensation of the fulness of times he might gather together in one all things in Christ, both which are in heaven, and which are on earth; *even* in him:

Rev 21:1 And I saw a new heaven and a new earth: for the first heaven and the first earth were passed away; and there was no more sea.

Rev 21:2 And I John saw the holy city, new Jerusalem, coming down from God out of heaven, prepared as a bride adorned for her husband.

Rev 21:3 And I heard a great voice out of heaven saying, Behold, the tabernacle of God *is* with men, and he will dwell with them, and they shall be his people, and God himself shall be with them, *and be* their God.

Rev 21:4 And God shall wipe away all tears from their eyes; and there shall be no more death, neither sorrow, nor crying, neither shall there be any more pain: for the former things are passed away.

Rev 21:5 And he that sat upon the throne said, Behold, I make all things new. And he said unto me, Write: for these words are true and faithful.

Rev 21:6 And he said unto me, It is done. I am Alpha and Omega, the beginning and the end. I will give unto him that is athirst of the fountain of the water of life freely.

Rev 21:7 He that overcometh shall inherit all things; and I will be his God, and he shall be my son.

Rev 21:9 And there came unto me one of the seven angels which had the seven vials full of the seven last plagues, and talked with me, saying, Come hither, I will shew thee the bride, the Lamb's wife.

Rev 21:10 And he carried me away in the spirit to a great and high mountain, and shewed me that great city, the holy Jerusalem, descending out of heaven from God,

Rev 22:1 And he shewed me a pure river of water of life, clear as crystal, proceeding out of the throne of God and of the Lamb.

Rev 22:2 In the midst of the street of it, and on either side of the river, *was there* the tree of life, which bare twelve *manner of* fruits, *and* yielded her fruit every month: and the leaves of the tree *were* for the healing of the nations.

Rev 22:3 And there shall be no more curse: but the throne of God and of the Lamb shall be in it; and his servants shall serve him:

Rev 22:4 And they shall see his face; and his name *shall be* in their foreheads.

Rev 22:5 And there shall be no night there; and they need no candle, neither light of the sun; for the Lord God giveth them light: and they shall reign for ever and ever.

The New Jerusalem

Scan Me!

Did you know?

> Exo 23:20 Behold, I send an Angel before thee, to keep thee in the way, and to bring thee into the place which I have prepared.

> Exo 23:21 Beware of him, and obey his voice, provoke him not; for he will not pardon your transgressions: for my name is in him.

> Exo 23:22 But if thou shalt indeed obey his voice, and do all that I speak; then I will be an enemy unto thine enemies, and an adversary unto thine adversaries.

This Angel was none other than Jesus Christ, before He became a man. In Moses' day He was known as Jehovah.

So we see 1 Jehovah sending another Jehovah to do His will (Guess that settles the question once and for all, there is more than 1 God taught in the Bible!)

Concerning this second person of the Trinity, He spent 40 years with the Jewish people in the wilderness. When He became a man, He spent 33 ½ years with them in Judea. When He comes back, He will spend another 1,000 years in Judea.

Finally, when the Father who sent Him to Earth in the first place comes and dwells with mankind for all eternity, Christ Jesus will still spend all eternity in Judea.

Now as for Born Again Christians, NOT one will spend eternity in Judea!

Nope, the Christian's home is with the Father in the New Jerusalem, and not the earthly Jerusalem in Israel.

The earthly Jerusalem will be the location of the earthly Capitol, while the New Jerusalem will be the location of the universal Capitol.

When all's said and done, and God finally moves the New Jerusalem to Earth, the remaining people of earth will be able to visit, but not live there, for flesh and blood does not inherit the Kingdom of God!

> 1Co_15:50 Now this I say, brethren, that flesh and blood cannot inherit the kingdom of God; neither doth corruption inherit incorruption.

A spiritual voyage into the pages of the Bible

Use this space for notes

What is Pentecost?

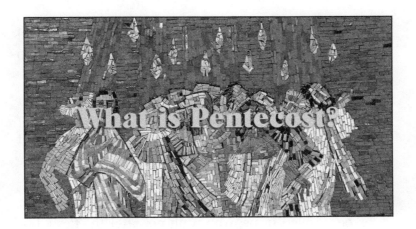

Scan Me!

There are tons of people who say they are Christians, but in fact there be just a few! If you are not walking in the Spirit, then you are just walking!

> Eze_36:27 And I will put my spirit within you, and cause you to walk in my statutes, and ye shall keep my judgments, and do *them*.

> Rom_8:1 *There is* therefore now no condemnation to them which are in Christ Jesus, who walk not after the flesh, but after the Spirit.

> Rom_8:4 That the righteousness of the law might be fulfilled in us, who walk not after the flesh, but after the Spirit.

> Gal_5:16 *This* I say then, Walk in the Spirit, and ye shall not fulfil the lust of the flesh.

> Gal_5:25 If we live in the Spirit, let us also walk in the Spirit.

> Luk 13:23 Then said one unto him, Lord, are there few that be saved? And he said unto them,

> Luk 13:24 Strive to enter in at the strait gate: for many, I say unto you, will seek to enter in, and shall not be able.

Luk 13:25 When once the master of the house is risen up, and hath shut to the door, and ye begin to stand without, and to knock at the door, saying, Lord, Lord, open unto us; and he shall answer and say unto you, I know you not whence ye are:

Luk 13:26 Then shall ye begin to say, We have eaten and drunk in thy presence, and thou hast taught in our streets.

Luk 13:27 But he shall say, I tell you, I know you not whence ye are; depart from me, all *ye* workers of iniquity.

Luk 13:28 There shall be weeping and gnashing of teeth, when ye shall see Abraham, and Isaac, and Jacob, and all the prophets, in the kingdom of God, and you *yourselves* thrust out.

Luk 13:29 And they shall come from the east, and *from* the west, and from the north, and *from* the south, and shall sit down in the kingdom of God.
Luk 13:30 And, behold, there are last which shall be first, and there are first which shall be last.

In order to walk after the Spirit, one must know who the Spirit is, and "No Virginia, the Holy Spirit is not Jesus Christ!" Never was, never will be!

Now about the Truth about the Baptism of the Holy Spirit!

Some general facts about the Spirit-Baptism;

1. That there is a Spirit Baptism, yet you don't need to be baptized in the Spirit to be saved.

2. Jesus was the first to be Baptized in the Spirit.

3. Baptism of the Holy Spirit was in fulfillment of prophecy.

4. Men in general were not baptised in the Spirit until Jesus was glorified and until Pentecost of that year 30 A.D.

Men/Women were "FILLED" or had "PORTIONS" of the Spirit in both Old and New Testament, but we only have records of men being Baptized in the Spirit in the New Testament.

The purpose of the Spirit baptism is to endue the believer with "POWER" to do the works of Christ.

The Spirit Baptism is the immersion or burial of the believer in the Spirit, at which time He receives the Spirit in his life in all fulness and without measure.

Most Born Again Christians are Spirit filled, yet not baptized in the Spirit.

Think of a "filling" and "baptism" as being illustrated by a glass (the believer) and water (the Holy Spirit.)

In a filling, the glass can be half filled, or fully filled, but now imagine taking that full glass of water and submerging it into a olympic sized pool, now the glass is considered as "without measure."

To get the Spirit Baptism, one must first be Born Again, and one has to "pray" to God the Father to be baptized in the Spirit. The Agent that baptises a believer in the Spirit is Jesus Christ, not your pastor!

You can ONLY say you are Baptized in the Spirit, when you "CAN DO THE WORKS OF CHRIST"!

Until that day, you are NOT baptized in the Holy Spirit. So strive for that day!

A spiritual voyage into the pages of the Bible

Use this space for notes

Chapter 3
Signs, Symbols, and
Types in the Bible

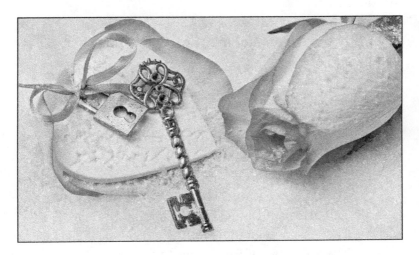

Biblical definition of "sign";

> G4592
> σημεῖον
> sēmeion
> say-mi'-on

Neuter of a presumed derivative of the base of G4591; an indication, especially ceremonially or supernaturally: - miracle, sign, token, wonder.

So think of a sign as a miracle, there are plenty of miracles in the Bible in both testaments. You can search for them yourself.

God produced miracles, and the future Antichrist will also produce miracles.

There are two sources for miracles, God and Lucifer.

Symbols of the Bible

There are a number of definite symbols in the Bible. Example of Biblical symbols are:

1) The image of Daniel chapter 2
2) The beasts of Daniel chapters 7 and 8; Rev. 13, 17
3) The 5 horsemen of Rev. 6
4) The 2 women of Rev. 12 and 17

Types in the Bible

All types are symbols, but not all symbols are types.

Types always refers to something future, and when the reality of the type comes to pass, then the type is no longer a type, but reality.

Example of a type of Christ: Joseph was a type of Christ, until Christ Jesus came.

The Aliens Among Us

Scan Me!

We are Aliens!

Rejoice!

How can you not rejoice if Jesus freely gave you His Joy?

God is an Alien, Jesus is an Alien, and those that follow Jesus are Aliens!

There is an old saying, "The Elohims are coming!"

Now the word Alien is an old Biblical word definition below:

גּר גיר

   gêr gêyr

   gare, gare

From H1481; properly a guest; by implication a foreigner: - alien, sojourner, stranger.
In Greek you have 2 definitions :

   ἀπαλλοτριόω

   apallotrioō
   ap-al-lot-ree-o'-o

From G575 and a derivative of G245; to estrange away, that is, (passively and figuratively) to be non participant:

- alienate, be alien.

ἀλλότριος

allotrios

al-lot'-ree-os

From G243; another's, that is, not one's own; by extension foreign, not akin, hostile: - alien, (an-) other (man's, men's), strange (-r).

Bottom line, the word Alien means a foreigner, a stranger.

The big question is what kind of Alien are you?

If you be of the world (Kosmos) then you are an Alien to God! That's not a good thing by the way!

If you be not of this world (Kosmos) then you are an Alien to the world, and thus the world HATES YOU! For you are an Alien to them! But yet God LOVES YOU for you are not an Alien to Him!

Jesus Himself said:

> Joh 18:36 **Jesus answered,** My kingdom is not of this world: if my kingdom were of this world, then would my servants fight, that I should not be delivered to the Jews: but now is my kingdom not from hence.

Biblical definition of "World"

kosmos

kos'-mos

Probably from the base of G2865; orderly arrangement, that is, decoration; by implication the world (in a wide or narrow sense, including its inhabitants, literally or figuratively [morally]): - adorning, world.

How did the Human race become Aliens to God?

Answer: SIN!

Sin is what has separated us from God, thus making us Aliens!

Jesus came into this world (Kosmos) Social order, to give us back our PASSPORTS, for it is written, you cannot get to the Father but by Me!

> Joh 14:6 **Jesus saith unto him,** I am the way, the truth, and the life: no man cometh unto the Father, but by me.

Rejoice! You have your Heavenly Passport!

This makes you a Citizen of the Holy City of God, The New Jerusalem, The bride of Christ!

The Holy City was a well known fact way back in the Old Testament.

> Heb 11:8 By faith Abraham, when he was called to go out into a place which he should after receive for an inheritance, obeyed; and he went out, not knowing whither he went.

> Heb 11:9 By faith he sojourned in the land of promise, as in a strange country, dwelling in tabernacles with Isaac and Jacob, the heirs with him of the same promise:

> Heb 11:10 For he looked for a city which hath foundations, whose builder and maker is God.

> Heb 11:11 Through faith also Sara herself received strength to conceive seed, and was delivered of a child when she was past age, because she judged him faithful who had promised.

> Heb 11:12 Therefore sprang there even of one, and him as good as dead, so many as the stars of the sky in multitude, and as the sand which is by the sea shore innumerable.

> Heb 11:13 These all died in faith, not having received the promises, but having seen them afar off, and were persuaded of them, and embraced them, and confessed that they were strangers and pilgrims on the earth.

Heb 11:14 For they that say such things declare plainly that they seek a country.

Heb 11:15 And truly, if they had been mindful of that country from whence they came out, they might have had opportunity to have returned.

Heb 11:16 But now they desire a better country, that is, an heavenly: wherefore God is not ashamed to be called their God: for he hath prepared for them a city.

Heb 12:22 But ye are come unto mount Sion, and unto the city of the living God, the heavenly Jerusalem, and to an innumerable company of angels,

Heb 12:23 To the general assembly and church of the firstborn, which are written in heaven, and to God the Judge of all, and to the spirits of just men made perfect,

Heb 13:14 For here have we no continuing city, but we seek one to come.

Rev 3:12 Him that overcometh will I make a pillar in the temple of my God, and he shall go no more out: and I will write upon him the name of my God, and the name of the city of my God, which is new Jerusalem, which cometh down out of heaven from my God: and I will write upon him my new name.

A spiritual voyage into the pages of the Bible

Rev 21:1 And I saw a new heaven and a new earth: for the first heaven and the first earth were passed away; and there was no more sea.

Rev 21:2 And I John saw the holy city, new Jerusalem, coming down from God out of heaven, prepared as a bride adorned for her husband.

Rev 22:5 And there shall be no night there; and they need no candle, neither light of the sun; for the Lord God giveth them light: and they shall reign for ever and ever.

So my fellow Alien I hope this helps you on your quest!

A spiritual voyage into the pages of the Bible

Use this space for notes

The Revelation 12 Sign

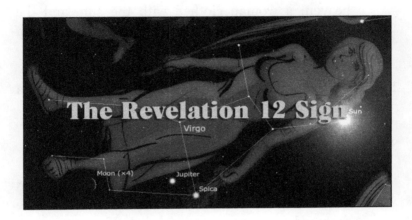

Scan Me!

The woman and child of Revelation 12:1 explained!

> Rev 12:1 And there appeared a great wonder in heaven; a woman clothed with the sun, and the moon under her feet, and upon her head a crown of twelve stars:

The woman is a symbol of national Israel, or Israel as a nation, they became the nation of Israel in 1948.

She was was introduced to us back in Gen. 37:9.

> Gen 37:9 And he dreamed yet another dream, and told it his brethren, and said, Behold, I have dreamed a dream more; and, behold, the sun and the moon and the eleven stars made obeisance to me.

The Sun represented Jacob (later God renamed him to Israel), the Moon his two wives, and the stars his sons.

> Rev 12:2 And she being with child cried, travailing in birth, and pained to be delivered.

The child represents the Firstborn of National Israel, meaning the 144,000 "Born Again" Jews in the tribulation period, they are also known as the Manchild!
Isaiah predicted this in his day!

> Isa 66:7 Before she travailed, she brought forth; before her pain came, she was delivered of a man child.

> Isa 66:8 Who hath heard such a thing? who hath seen such things? Shall the earth be made to bring forth in one day? or shall a nation be born at once? for as soon as Zion travailed, she brought forth her children.

In verse 5 of Revelation you will read that the child was "Caught up unto God.." meaning they will be Raptured just before the last 3 ½ years of the tribulation period.

> Rev 12:5 And she brought forth a man child, who was to rule all nations with a rod of iron: and her child was caught up unto God, and *to* his throne.

In verse 6 you will notice the woman fled into the wilderness, and that means the rest of the Jews fled to Petra the rock city, where they are protected for the last 3 ½ years of the tribulation period.

> Rev 12:6 And the woman fled into the wilderness, where she hath a place prepared of God, that they should feed her there a thousand two hundred *and* threescore days.

As of this writing, the "prophesied" date of September 23, 2017 for the start of the tribulation, declared by many false teachers came and went! (Nothing happened BTW)

So there you have the truth about who the woman and child are in Revelation 12!

Jesus Was Not Born On December 25

Scan Me!

Throughout the Bible, we see examples of how God instituted holidays and observances on specific days of the calendar. In order to ensure that the Israelites didn't forget which days those events were to occur on, he gave specific signs to look for. Namely, waiting for a full or New Moon on a specific day and month.

Failure to remember these dates would result in lost blessings to the individual or nation, and would sometimes result in death!

> Num 15:32 And while the children of Israel were in the wilderness, they found a man that gathered sticks upon the sabbath day.
>
> Num 15:33 And they that found him gathering sticks brought him unto Moses and Aaron, and unto all the congregation.
>
> Num 15:34 And they put him in ward, because it was not declared what should be done to him.
>
> Num 15:35 And the LORD said unto Moses, The man shall be surely put to death: all the congregation shall stone him with stones without the camp.
>
> Num 15:36 And all the congregation brought him without the camp, and stoned him with stones, and he died; as the LORD commanded Moses.

Num 15:37 And the LORD spake unto Moses, saying,

Num 15:38 Speak unto the children of Israel, and bid them that they make them fringes in the borders of their garments throughout their generations, and that they put upon the fringe of the borders a ribband of blue:

Num 15:39 And it shall be unto you for a fringe, that ye may look upon it, and remember all the commandments of the LORD, and do them; and that ye seek not after your own heart and your own eyes, after which ye use to go a whoring:

Num 15:40 That ye may remember, and do all my commandments, and be holy unto your God.

Num 15:41 I am the LORD your God, which brought you out of the land of Egypt, to be your God: I am the LORD your God.

Ouch! The difference for this poor man between life and death was hours, or one day. Maybe he forgot, or was distracted, or just followed someone else's advice about where and how to gather firewood so he could prepare a nice hot meal to go for his family. We will never know why, but the end result displeased God, and he had to make an example of him.

God takes his special days seriously!

He's not alone. Many of us take the most important day of our lives rather seriously too. Our birthday!

Many go out of their way to make sure friends and family remember the day they were born. If you want to upset your best friend or family member don't do anything on their birthday! In fact, ignore it completely as if it was just an ordinary day. If you feel suicidal, forget your spouse's birthday or wedding anniversary!

Chances are the person celebrating their special day will feel more than just a little upset with you. To rub more salt in the wound, pick any other day, months away from the actual date, and use that day to celebrate their birthday, anniversary or memorial.

If you've ever had this happen to you, it's not a good feeling at all. So in a way, we can imagine how God feels when he's done so much for us, and we don't honor Him the way we should, especially when we remember to celebrate people around us who might not always be there for us in our time of need.

Every December 25th, people all around the world get together to celebrate Christ Jesus' birthday. Big preparations are made, presents are bought to exchange or give to the special people in their lives, some businesses close their operations and give a bonus paycheck to those that have to work that day. Christmas is a big holiday.

Even many non-Christians get in the holiday mood. Jews, Muslims, atheists get into the holiday cheer by going against family traditions and getting into the merrymaking that usually lasts the week of Christmas up until New Year's Day on January 1st.

But what does the Bible say about celebrating Christmas? Is there a date given for Jesus' birthday, and if so, is there a special way or command to celebrate it?

Well, in case you didn't know, the idea of Christmas is not new. It is a very old tradition that dates back thousands of years before Jesus was born.

The first mention of this holiday can be found in the book of Jeremiah.

> Jer 10:1 Hear ye the word which the LORD speaketh unto you, O house of Israel:

> Jer 10:2 Thus saith the LORD, Learn not the way of the heathen, and be not dismayed at the signs of heaven; for the heathen are dismayed at them.

> Jer 10:3 For the customs of the people are vain: for one cutteth a tree out of the forest, the work of the hands of the workman, with the axe.

> Jer 10:4 They deck it with silver and with gold; they fasten it with nails and with hammers, that it move not.

Jer 10:5 They are upright as the palm tree, but speak not: they must needs be borne, because they cannot go. Be not afraid of them; for they cannot do evil, neither also is it in them to do good.

Jer 10:6 Forasmuch as there is none like unto thee, O LORD; thou art great, and thy name is great in might.

Nowhere in the Bible is it written that we are commanded to observe anyone's birthday!

As a matter of fact, the word "birthday" is mentioned only 3 times in the entire Bible, and in each case, someone lost their heads during the "celebrations"!

Gen 40:20 And it came to pass the third day, which was Pharaoh's birthday, that he made a feast unto all his servants: and he lifted up the head of the chief butler and of the chief baker among his servants.

Mat 14:6 But when Herod's birthday was kept, the daughter of Herodias danced before them, and pleased Herod.

Mar 6:21 And when a convenient day was come, that Herod on his birthday made a supper to his lords, high captains, and chief estates of Galilee;

Mar 6:22 And when the daughter of the said Herodias came in, and danced, and pleased Herod and them that sat with him, the king said unto the damsel, Ask of me whatsoever thou wilt, and I will give it thee.

Mar 6:23 And he sware unto her, Whatsoever thou shalt ask of me, I will give it thee, unto the half of my kingdom.

Mar 6:24 And she went forth, and said unto her mother, What shall I ask? And she said, The head of John the Baptist.

Personal note: This must be the reason why I never enjoyed celebrating birthdays, be it mine or for someone else!

Not such a fun way to celebrate a birthday if you ask me!

So, how did we get to celebrate Jesus' birthday on December 25th of every year? Do we know for a fact that on this day some 2,000 years ago Christ was born? And why is the date for celebrating his death (Easter) fall on a different date every year, but not his birthday?

Well, to find out when Jesus' actual birth date is, we need the help of his cousin, the aforementioned John the Baptist!

A spiritual voyage into the pages of the Bible

Luk 1:5 There was in the days of Herod, the king of Judaea, a certain priest named Zacharias, of the course of Abia: and his wife was of the daughters of Aaron, and her name was Elisabeth.

Luk 1:8 And it came to pass, that while he executed the priest's office before God in the order of his course,

Luk 1:9 According to the custom of the priest's office, his lot was to burn incense when he went into the temple of the Lord.

Luk 1:11 And there appeared unto him an angel of the Lord standing on the right side of the altar of incense.

Luk 1:13 But the angel said unto him, Fear not, Zacharias: for thy prayer is heard; and thy wife Elisabeth shall bear thee a son, and thou shalt call his name John.

Luk 1:23 And it came to pass, that, as soon as the days of his ministration were accomplished, he departed to his own house.

Luk 1:24 And after those days his wife Elisabeth conceived, and hid herself five months, saying,

Luk 1:25 Thus hath the Lord dealt with me in the days wherein he looked on me, to take away my reproach among men.

From these verses, we see that John the Baptist's father, Zacharias was a priest, of the order Abia (Abijah), and that it was his turn to perform services at the temple for that specific month.

In the book of 1 Chronicles chapters 24 and 28, King David establishes the duty roster for all the priests that are to perform services in the temple. In all, there were 24 priests that had to perform regular weekly services every Shabbos. This would require them to perform 2 tours of duty within the calendar year.

In addition to this, all the priests (Kohanim) were required to assemble 3 times per year for the high holidays of the Feast of Unleavened bread, Pentecost (Shavuot) and the Feast of Tabernacles.

In total, Zacharias had 5 tours of duty in the temple per year. His order was that of Abijah, which was the 8th place out of the 24.

The month of Nisan is the 1st month of the religious calendar (March/April), while Rosh Hashanah is the date for the civil new year, which occurs in September/October of every year).

Table 1 illustrates the timing of the priestly order up until the month that Zacharias was to perform his duties:

Table 1: Priestly order

Secular month	March/April	April/May	May/June
Hebrew month	(Abib/Nisan)	Zif/Iyyar	Sivan
Week 1	Jehoiarib #1	Seorim #4	*Pentecost*
Week 2	Jedaiah #2	Malchijah #5	**Abijah #8**
Week 3	*Unleavened Bread*	Mijamin #6	Jeshuah #9
Week 4	Harim #3	Hakkoz #7	Shecaniah #10

When it was announced that Elizabeth was pregnant with John, he had just finished his tour at the temple (Luk 1:9).

The key is found in the New Testament in the Gospel of Luke.

Here is the key!

> Luk 1:5 There was in the days of Herod, the king of Judaea, a certain priest named Zacharias, of the course of Abia: and his wife *was* of the daughters of Aaron, and her name *was* Elisabeth.

"Abia" it all comes down to the course of Abia in timing John's birthday.

Once his duties were finished, he went back home with Elizabeth. John was conceived shortly thereafter.

Elizabeth remained out of sight for at least 5 months (Luk 1:24).

The following month (or the 6th month of Elizabeth's pregnancy), her cousin Mary received the news from the angel Gabriel that she would soon conceive a child, by the power of the Holy Spirit, and would name him Jesus (Luk 1:31).

Mary was even informed that her cousin was already 6 months pregnant.

> Luk 1:36 And, behold, thy cousin Elisabeth, she hath also conceived a son in her old age: and this is the sixth month with her, who was called barren.

Putting the dates into context here, we see that John the Baptist was conceived sometime in June/July. 40 weeks later he would be born which would be sometime in the month of March/April which is when Passover occurs.

> Mal 3:1 Behold, I will send my messenger (John the Baptist), and he shall prepare the way before me: and the Lord, whom ye seek, shall suddenly come to his temple, even the messenger of the covenant, whom ye delight in: behold, he shall come, saith the LORD of hosts.

The Old Testament prophet Malachi was told that Elijah would be sent out before the LORD's Second Advent.
This prophecy has yet to take place!

Mal 4:5 Behold, I will send you Elijah the prophet before the coming of the great and dreadful day of the LORD:

Mal 4:6 And he shall turn the heart of the fathers to the children, and the heart of the children to their fathers, lest I come and smite the earth with a curse.

And Jesus said of John that he was the "Elijah" to come, but he came and went and no one noticed.

Mat 17:12 But I say unto you, That Elias is come already, and they knew him not, but have done unto him whatsoever they listed. Likewise shall also the Son of man suffer of them.

Mat 17:13 Then the disciples understood that he spake unto them of John the Baptist.

Mary began her conception 6 months after Elizabeth began hers, which places Mary's conception date sometime in early December, at around the time of Chanukah, or the festival of lights. 40 weeks later Jesus would be born, which would be sometime in September/October, at around the time of the Feast of Tabernacles.

It is interesting to note that the prophet Zechariah declared that after the 7-year tribulation, all the remaining nations on Earth must go to Jerusalem to worship the King, Jesus....on His Birthday!

> Zec 14:16 And it shall come to pass, that every one that is left of all the nations which came against Jerusalem shall even go up from year to year to worship the King, the LORD of hosts, and to keep the feast of tabernacles.

Your presence will be required!

> Zec 14:17 And it shall be, that whoso will not come up of all the families of the earth unto Jerusalem to worship the King, the LORD of hosts, even upon them shall be no rain.

So why the December 25th date, the stories of Saint Nick, reindeer, mistletoe, the drunken office parties, and all the familiar traditions we blindly keep year after year at Christmas time?

Well, according to some old traditions, ancient peoples needed to know when to plant and harvest crops. This meant life or death for an entire village.

They noticed that at a certain time of the year, it appeared as though the sun stopped moving in the sky, reaching its lowest point on the horizon for 3 days. This was known as the winter solstice, which occurs around December 21-24.

Gradually over time, the customs involved being festive for the entire month of December, which saw citizens indulge in what amounts to sex, drugs and rock n roll, where anything and everything were permitted.

The Romans took this to the next level, and in order to maintain order within their empire, they incorporated Christianity into their secular pagan festival of Saturnalia, Easter and many other holidays which date back to the days of Nimrod in Genesis 10:8,9 ; which was a shadow of Lucifer's reign in the pre-Adamite days.

The Christmas as you know it today has nothing at all to do with Jesus, or any Jewish custom for that matter. It is pagan, and an abomination to the Gods, and honors the god of this world, in all his forms, Satan.

Be different. Stop being a sheep following traditions that will only lead you to hell!

BTW Jesus was not given any gifts when He was born, the wise men only brought Him gifts later on about 2 years later when He was home with Mary his mother!

So make a difference this holiday season by taking Santa Claus out of your children's lives, and tell them the truth of the wonderful gift that God gave Mary and to this world, Who was conceived on the festival of lights, and born on the first day of Sukkot which is the 15th of Tishri!

Joh 8:12 **Then spake Jesus again unto them, saying,** I am the light of the world: he that followeth me shall not walk in darkness, but shall have the light of life.

A spiritual voyage into the pages of the Bible

Use this space for notes

Christians and the Sabbath

Scan Me!

Sabbath keeping is no longer a requirement for salvation!

Deu 5:15 And remember that thou wast a servant in the land of Egypt, and that the LORD thy God brought thee out thence through a mighty hand and by a stretched out arm: therefore the LORD thy God commanded thee to keep the sabbath day.

Gal 3:1 O foolish Galatians, who hath bewitched you, that ye should not obey the truth, before whose eyes Jesus Christ hath been evidently set forth, crucified among you?

Gal 3:2 This only would I learn of you, Received ye the Spirit by the works of the law, or by the hearing of faith?

Gal 3:3 Are ye so foolish? having begun in the Spirit, are ye now made perfect by the flesh?

Gal 3:17 And this I say, that the covenant, that was confirmed before of God in Christ, the law, which was four hundred and thirty years after, cannot disannul, that it should make the promise of none effect.

Gal 3:18 For if the inheritance be of the law, it is no more of promise: but God gave it to Abraham by promise.

Gal 3:19 Wherefore then serveth the law? It was added because of transgressions, till the seed should come to whom the promise was made; and it was ordained by angels in the hand of a mediator.

Gal 3:20 Now a mediator is not a mediator of one, but God is one.

Gal 3:21 Is the law then against the promises of God? God forbid: for if there had been a law given which could have given life, verily righteousness should have been by the law.

Gal 3:22 But the scripture hath concluded all under sin, that the promise by faith of Jesus Christ might be given to them that believe.

Gal 3:23 But before faith came, we were kept under the law, shut up unto the faith which should afterwards be revealed.

Gal 3:24 Wherefore the law was our schoolmaster to bring us unto Christ, that we might be justified by faith.

Gal 3:25 But after that faith is come, we are no longer under a schoolmaster.

Gal 3:26 For ye are all the children of God by faith in Christ Jesus.

Mat_6:5 And when thou prayest, thou shalt not be as the hypocrites are: for they love to pray standing in the synagogues and in the corners of the streets, that they may be seen of men. Verily I say unto you, They have their reward.

Mat_23:13 But woe unto you, scribes and Pharisees, hypocrites! for ye shut up the kingdom of heaven against men: for ye neither go in yourselves, neither suffer ye them that are entering to go in.

Mat_23:15 Woe unto you, scribes and Pharisees, hypocrites! for ye compass sea and land to make one proselyte, and when he is made, ye make him twofold more the child of hell than yourselves.

The Jews have 613 commandments (mitzvot) and Christians have about 1,050 and the only one that did not make it into the New Testament was the "KEEPING of the SABBATH DAY!"

BTW!

To keep the Sabbath day, make sure you follow the whole commandment, meaning get ready for a 6 day work week!

Else my friend, you have sinned!

Gospel in the Stars

Scan Me!

Israel will not listen to the 144,000 born again Jews. The main reason is that during the first part of the tribulation Israel will accept the Antichrist as their Messiah, then at midweek he will turn on them. By then the 144,000 will be in Heaven.

Who will guide them when the "Manchild" is gone?

Elijah and Enoch! The last 2 wilderness prophets.

Moses and Aaron were the first 2 wilderness prophets.

Like Moses and Aaron, Elijah and Enoch will protect the Jews and lead them to Petra, Sela, Bozrah, call it what you will, it is the rock city where Christ will do His flyby.

> Isa 42:11 Let the wilderness and the cities thereof lift up their voice, the villages that Kedar doth inhabit: let the inhabitants of the rock sing, let them shout from the top of the mountains.

> Eze 20:33 As I live, saith the Lord GOD, surely with a mighty hand, and with a stretched out arm, and with fury poured out, will I rule over you:

> Eze 20:34 And I will bring you out from the people, and will gather you out of the countries wherein ye are scattered, with a mighty hand, and with a stretched out arm, and with fury poured out.

Eze 20:35 And I will bring you into the wilderness of the people, and there will I plead with you face to face.

Eze 20:36 Like as I pleaded with your fathers in the wilderness of the land of Egypt, so will I plead with you, saith the Lord GOD.

Eze 20:37 And I will cause you to pass under the rod, and I will bring you into the bond of the covenant:

Eze 20:38 And I will purge out from among you the rebels, and them that transgress against me: I will bring them forth out of the country where they sojourn, and they shall not enter into the land of Israel: and ye shall know that I am the LORD.

Mal 4:4 Remember ye the law of Moses my servant, which I commanded unto him in Horeb for all Israel, with the statutes and judgments.

Mal 4:5 Behold, I will send you Elijah the prophet before the coming of the great and dreadful day of the LORD:

Rev 11:3 And I will give power unto my two witnesses, and they shall prophesy a thousand two hundred and threescore days, clothed in sackcloth.

Rev 11:4 These are the two olive trees, and the two candlesticks standing before the God of the earth.

Zechariah did not know who they were!

Zec 4:11 Then answered I, and said unto him, What are these two olive trees upon the right side of the candlestick and upon the left side thereof?

Zec 4:12 And I answered again, and said unto him, What be these two olive branches which through the two golden pipes empty the golden oil out of themselves?

Zec 4:13 And he answered me and said, Knowest thou not what these be? And I said, No, my lord.

Zec 4:14 Then said he, These are the two anointed ones, that stand by the Lord of the whole earth.

Rev 11:5 And if any man will hurt them, fire proceedeth out of their mouth, and devoureth their enemies: and if any man will hurt them, he must in this manner be killed.

Rev 11:6 These have power to shut heaven, that it rain not in the days of their prophecy: and have power over waters to turn them to blood, and to smite the earth with all plagues, as often as they will.

Rev 11:7 And when they shall have finished their testimony, the beast that ascendeth out of the bottomless pit shall make war against them, and shall overcome them, and kill them.

Rev 11:8 And their dead bodies shall lie in the street of the great city, which spiritually is called Sodom and Egypt, where also our Lord was crucified.

Rev 11:9 And they of the people and kindreds and tongues and nations shall see their dead bodies three days and an half, and shall not suffer their dead bodies to be put in graves.

Rev 11:10 And they that dwell upon the earth shall rejoice over them, and make merry, and shall send gifts one to another; because these two prophets tormented them that dwelt on the earth.

Rev 11:11 And after three days and an half the Spirit of life from God entered into them, and they stood upon their feet; and great fear fell upon them which saw them.

Rev 11:12 And they heard a great voice from heaven saying unto them, Come up hither. And they ascended up to heaven in a cloud; and their enemies beheld them.

Rev 11:13   And the same hour was there a great earthquake, and the tenth part of the city fell, and in the earthquake were slain of men seven thousand: and the remnant were affrighted, and gave glory to the God of heaven.

Also, like Moses and Aaron did not bring the Children of Israel into the promised land, but that task was left to Joshua, so will it be with the end time return. This time Jesus will bring them into their promised land.

Jesus is the English name of the Hebrew name Joshua, which means: Jehovah-saved.

Do You Have Faith?

Scan Me!

Do you Believe?

> Heb 11:1 Now faith is the substance of things hoped for, the evidence of things not seen.

> Heb 11:2 For by it the elders obtained a good report.

Faith a requirement!

> Heb 11:6 But without faith it is impossible to please him: for he that cometh to God must believe that he is, and that he is a rewarder of them that diligently seek him.

ASK in Faith!

> Jas 1:6 But let him ask in faith, nothing wavering. For he that wavereth is like a wave of the sea driven with the wind and tossed.

> Jas 1:7 For let not that man think that he shall receive anything of the Lord.

> Jas 1:8 A double minded man is unstable in all his ways.

Don't be rebuked by Christ Jesus!

He even had to rebuke His own Disciples!

> Mat_17:17 Then Jesus answered and said, O faithless and perverse generation, how long shall I be with you? how long shall I suffer you? bring him hither to me.

Mar_9:19 **He answereth him, and saith,** O faithless generation, how long shall I be with you? how long shall I suffer you? bring him unto me.

Luk_9:41 **And Jesus answering said,** O faithless and perverse generation, how long shall I be with you, and suffer you? Bring thy son hither.

Joh_20:27 **Then saith he to Thomas,** Reach hither thy finger, and behold my hands; and reach hither thy hand, and thrust it into my side: and be not faithless, but believing.

Mar 16:14 **Afterward he appeared unto the eleven as they sat at meat, and upbraided them with their unbelief and hardness of heart, because they believed not them which had seen him after he was risen.**

Mar 16:15 **And he said unto them,** Go ye into all the world, and preach the gospel to every creature.

Mar 16:16 He that believeth and is baptized shall be saved; but he that believeth not shall be damned.

A spiritual voyage into the pages of the Bible

Use this space for notes

Antichrist: The Little Horn

Scan Me!

A spiritual voyage into the pages of the Bible

The number of the beast,

666

and what will the Beast call himself?

The Number is rendered in Greek numerical form:

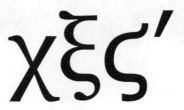

"Christ" in Greek is Χ ριστο ς (Christos)

Rev 13:1 And I stood upon the sand of the sea, and saw a beast rise up out of the sea, having seven heads and ten horns, and upon his horns ten crowns, and upon his heads the name of blasphemy.

What is the name of "blasphemy"?

Dictionary definition of blasphemy:

1. A contemptuous or profane act, utterance, or writing concerning God or a sacred entity.

2. The act of claiming for oneself the attributes and rights of God.

Well look at what the Bible says:

Mat 26:63 But Jesus held his peace. And the high priest answered and said unto him, I adjure thee by the living God, that thou tell us whether thou be the Christ, the Son of God.

Mat 26:64 **Jesus saith unto him,** Thou hast said: nevertheless I say unto you, Hereafter shall ye see the Son of man sitting on the right hand of power, and coming in the clouds of heaven.

Mat 26:65 Then the high priest rent his clothes, saying, He hath spoken blasphemy; what further need have we of witnesses? behold, now ye have heard his blasphemy.

Joh 10:33 The Jews answered him, saying, For a good work we stone thee not; but for blasphemy; and because that thou, being a man, makest thyself God.

The Jews rejected the real Christ, yet will accept this so called Christ/Messiah!

> Joh 5:43 I am come in my Father's name, and ye receive me not: if another shall come in his own name, him ye will receive.

This world ruler will call himself

"CHRIST"

This is the whole point of the Rapture, for NO Christian on Earth would keep quiet about this FALSE Christ!

> Rev 13:18 Here is wisdom. Let him that hath understanding count the number of the beast: for it is the number of a man; and his number *is* Six hundred threescore *and* six.

John knew, for Jesus taught it, now the question is did you pay attention?

> Mat 24:3 And as he sat upon the mount of Olives, the disciples came unto him privately, saying, Tell us, when shall these things be? and what *shall be* the sign of thy coming, and of the end of the world?

Mat 24:4 **And Jesus answered and said unto them,** Take heed that no man deceive you.

Mat 24:5 For many shall come in my name, saying, I am Christ; and shall deceive many.

Mat 24:6 And ye shall hear of wars and rumours of wars: see that ye be not troubled: for all *these things* must come to pass, but the end is not yet.

Mat 24:7 For nation shall rise against nation, and kingdom against kingdom: and there shall be famines, and pestilences, and earthquakes, in divers places.

Mat 24:8 All these *are* the beginning of sorrows.

Mat 24:9 Then shall they deliver you up to be afflicted, and shall kill you: and ye shall be hated of all nations for my name's sake.

Mat 24:10 And then shall many be offended, and shall betray one another, and shall hate one another.

Mat 24:11 And many false prophets shall rise, and shall deceive many.

Mat 24:12 And because iniquity shall abound, the love of many shall wax cold.

Mat 24:13 But he that shall endure unto the end, the same shall be saved.

Mat 24:14 And this gospel of the kingdom shall be preached in all the world for a witness unto all nations; and then shall the end come.

Mat 24:15   When ye therefore shall see the abomination of desolation, spoken of by Daniel the prophet, stand in the holy place, (whoso readeth, let him understand:)

Mat 24:16 Then let them which be in Judaea flee into the mountains:

Mat 24:17 Let him which is on the housetop not come down to take any thing out of his house:

Mat 24:18 Neither let him which is in the field return back to take his clothes.

Mat 24:19 And woe unto them that are with child, and to them that give suck in those days!

Mat 24:20 But pray ye that your flight be not in the winter, neither on the sabbath day:

Mat 24:21 For then shall be great tribulation, such as was not since the beginning of the world to this time, no, nor ever shall be.

Mat 24:22   And except those days should be shortened, there should no flesh be saved: but for the elect's sake those days shall be shortened.

Mat 24:23 Then if any man shall say unto you, Lo, here *is* Christ, or there; believe *it* not.

Mat 24:24 For there shall arise false Christs, and false prophets, and shall shew great signs and wonders; insomuch that, if *it were* possible, they shall deceive the very elect.

Mat 24:25 Behold, I have told you before.

Mat 24:26 Wherefore if they shall say unto you, Behold, he is in the desert; go not forth: behold, *he is* in the secret chambers; believe *it* not.

Mat 24:27 For as the lightning cometh out of the east, and shineth even unto the west; so shall also the coming of the Son of man be.

Mat 24:28 For wheresoever the carcase is, there will the eagles be gathered together.

Mat 24:29 Immediately after the tribulation of those days shall the sun be darkened, and the moon shall not give her light, and the stars shall fall from heaven, and the powers of the heavens shall be shaken:

2Th 2:3 Let no man deceive you by any means: for *that day shall not come,* except there come a falling away first, and that man of sin be revealed, the son of perdition;

2Th 2:4 Who opposeth and exalteth himself above all that is called God, or that is worshipped; so that he as God sitteth in the temple of God, shewing himself that he is God.

2Th 2:5 Remember ye not, that, when I was yet with you, I told you these things?

2Th 2:6 And now ye know what withholdeth that he might be revealed in his time.

2Th 2:7 For the mystery of iniquity doth already work: only he who now letteth *will let,* until he be taken out of the way.

2Th 2:8 And then shall that Wicked be revealed, whom the Lord shall consume with the spirit of his mouth, and shall destroy with the brightness of his coming:

2Th 2:9 *Even him,* whose coming is after the working of Satan with all power and signs and lying wonders,

Rev 14:9 And the third angel followed them, saying with a loud voice, If any man worship the beast and his image, and receive *his* mark in his forehead, or in his hand,

Rev 14:10 The same shall drink of the wine of the wrath of God, which is poured out without mixture into the cup of his indignation; and he shall be tormented with fire and brimstone in the presence of the holy angels, and in the presence of the Lamb:

Rev 14:11   And the smoke of their torment ascendeth up for ever and ever: and they have no rest day nor night, who worship the beast and his image, and whosoever receiveth the mark of his name.

Rev 19:20   And the beast was taken, and with him the false prophet that wrought miracles before him, with which he deceived them that had received the mark of the beast, and them that worshipped his image. These both were cast alive into a lake of fire burning with brimstone.

Dan 12:7   And I heard the man clothed in linen, which *was* upon the waters of the river, when he held up his right hand and his left hand unto heaven, and sware by him that liveth for ever that *it shall be* for a time, times, and an half; and when he shall have accomplished to scatter the power of the holy people, all these *things* shall be finished.

Dan 12:8   And I heard, but I understood not: then said I, O my Lord, what *shall be* the end of these *things?*

Dan 12:9   And he said, Go thy way, Daniel: for the words *are* closed up and sealed till the time of the end.

Dan 12:10   Many shall be purified, and made white, and tried; but the wicked shall do wickedly: and none of the wicked shall understand; but the wise shall understand.

> Dan 12:11   And from the time *that* the daily *sacrifice* shall be taken away, and the abomination that maketh desolate set up, *there shall be* a thousand two hundred and ninety days.

> Rev 6:2   And I saw, and behold a white horse: and he that sat on him had a bow; and a crown was given unto him: and he went forth conquering, and to conquer.

Who are the Jews waiting for? The Messiah, which in Greek is Christo, and Christ in English!

Anyone against Christ is an antichrist. In this sense there are now many antichrists, but the one referred to in the Bible focuses on the one yet to come.

He has several Biblical names below is a list.

1. Antichrist

2. The Assyrian

3. The King of Babylon

4. The Spoiler

5. The Extortioner

6. Gog, the Chief Prince of Meschech and Tubal

7. The Little Horn

8. King of Fierce Countenance

9. The King of the North

10. The Man of Sin

11. The Son of Perdition

12. The Wicked

13. That Wicked

14. The Beast

15. The Little Horn

But calling himself Christ will be his biggest mistake!

> Exo 34:14 For thou shalt worship no other god: for the LORD, whose name *is* Jealous, *is* a jealous God:

Remember Herod's death, why was he struck down?

The answer is in the Book of Acts!

> Act 12:21 And upon a set day Herod, arrayed in royal apparel, sat upon his throne, and made an oration unto them.

Act 12:22 And the people gave a shout, saying, It is the voice of a god, and not of a man.

Act 12:23 And immediately the angel of the Lord smote him, because he gave not God the glory: and he was eaten of worms, and gave up the ghost.

Chapter 4
Becoming a New Creature

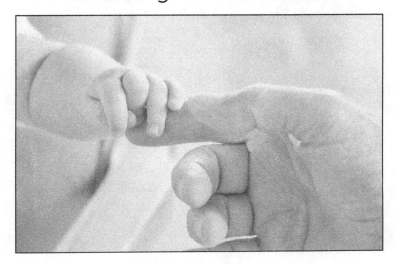

Joh_3:3 **Jesus answered and said unto him,** Verily, verily, I say unto thee, Except a man be born again, he cannot see the kingdom of God.

Joh_3:7 Marvel not that I said unto thee, Ye must be born again.

1Pe_1:23 **Being born again, not of corruptible seed, but of incorruptible, by the word of God,** which liveth and abideth for ever.

Being born again not physically but spiritually.

So when Jesus revealed this mystery to a Rabbi, he was basically telling him that he was spiritually dead!

All those years reading the Talmud did not qualify that Rabbi to see the Kingdom of God!

A spiritual voyage into the pages of the Bible

The Holy Spirit: First Contact

Scan Me!

A spiritual voyage into the pages of the Bible

The Holy Spirit is a God!

He is a real person separate and distinct from both the
Father and the Son.

He is an individual member of the Godhead or Deity, and
He has a separate body, soul, and spirit from both the
Father and the Son.

He is known as the 3rd person of the Divine Trinity, He is
called Holy Ghost and Holy Spirit about 97 times in both
testaments.

There are over 20 Divine names and titles ascribed to Him.

Now read the following very slowly and see for yourself!

> 1Co 12:1 Now concerning spiritual *gifts,* brethren, I
> would not have you ignorant.

> 1Co 12:2 Ye know that ye were Gentiles, carried
> away unto these dumb idols, even as ye were led.

> 1Co 12:3 Wherefore I give you to understand, that
> no man speaking by the Spirit of God calleth Jesus
> accursed: and *that* no man can say that Jesus is the
> Lord, but by the Holy Ghost.

> 1Co 12:4 Now there are diversities of gifts, but the
> same Spirit.

1Co 12:5   And there are differences of administrations, but the same Lord.

1Co 12:6 And there are diversities of operations, but it is the same God which worketh all in all.

1Co 12:7 But the manifestation of the Spirit is given to every man to profit withal.

1Co 12:8 For to one is given by the Spirit the word of wisdom; to another the word of knowledge by the same Spirit;

1Co 12:9 To another faith by the same Spirit; to another the gifts of healing by the same Spirit;

1Co 12:10 To another the working of miracles; to another prophecy; to another discerning of spirits; to another *divers* kinds of tongues; to another the interpretation of tongues:

1Co 12:11 But all these worketh that one and the selfsame Spirit, dividing to every man severally as he will.

1Co 12:12 For as the body is one, and hath many members, and all the members of that one body, being many, are one body: so also *is* Christ.

> 1Co 12:13   For by one Spirit are we all baptized into one body, whether *we be* Jews or Gentiles, whether *we be* bond or free; and have been all made to drink into one Spirit.

V3 He is called the Spirit of God.

V3 He is called Holy Ghost.

V4 Same Spirit as the 2 named in verse 3.

V5 He is called Lord.

V6 He is called God.

This is what Peter revealed to Ananias in the verses below. He told him he did not lie to man, but to the Holy Ghost, unto God.

So Peter knew the difference between the 3 members of the Godhead!

> Act 5:3   But Peter said, Ananias, why hath Satan filled thine heart to lie to the Holy Ghost, and to keep back *part* of the price of the land?

> Act 5:4   Whiles it remained, was it not thine own? and after it was sold, was it not in thine own power? why hast thou conceived this thing in thine heart? thou hast not lied unto men, but unto God.

The Holy Spirit is the Author of the new birth and the Direct Executive of God in all phases of creation and redemption.

As a real person the Holy Spirit does not live in born again Christians bodies, he is not a demon to bodily enter into people, the only way the Holy Spirit enters into man is in the form of "In union with".

In Genesis we read in the Hebrew text that Elohim created the heaven and the earth.

The word for God in Genesis 1:1 is Elohim which is plural for Gods.

He is first mentioned by name in verse 2!

> And the Spirit of God moved upon the face of the waters.

He is called the Comforter and Helper and Guide of all Saints. He is the Convictor of sin, the Power of God on earth, the Great Teacher of men, the Preserver of all things, the Chief Witness of God on earth, the Healer of Saints, the Inspirer of the Holy Scriptures, the Bestower of Spiritual gifts and the Character builder.

Personal names are given to Him.

Personal pronouns are used of Him.

Personal attributes are ascribed to Him.

Personal works are ascribed to Him.

Personal references are made concerning Him.

Personal treatment is ascribed to Him.

> Joh 15:26 But when the Comforter is come, whom I will send unto you from the Father, *even* the Spirit of truth, which proceedeth from the Father, he shall testify of me:

In John the Holy Spirit is spoken of as "ANOTHER" Comforter, who could not be sent until Christ had gone back to Heaven and was glorified, but would then be sent as a separate person from the Father and the Son.

The Spirit is "ANOTHER" from the Son who promised Him, and "ANOTHER" from the Father who sent Him.

Watch what you say about Him!

Blasphemy against the Son of God can be forgiven, yet Blasphemy against the Holy Ghost **will not be forgiven**!

Mat 12:31 Wherefore I say unto you, All manner of sin and blasphemy shall be forgiven unto men: but the blasphemy *against* the *Holy* Ghost shall not be forgiven unto men.

Mat 12:32 And whosoever speaketh a word against the Son of man, it shall be forgiven him: but whosoever speaketh against the Holy Ghost, it shall not be forgiven him, neither in this world, neither in the *world* to come.

If you love to read the Bible know that He is the Ghost Writer of the Scriptures. He inspired many men over the centuries to pen down what we call today the Word of God.

So I leave you with this.

Eph_6:17 And take the helmet of salvation, and the sword of the Spirit, which is the word of God:

A spiritual voyage into the pages of the Bible

Use this space for notes

A spiritual voyage into the pages of the Bible

The Cure for Anxiety

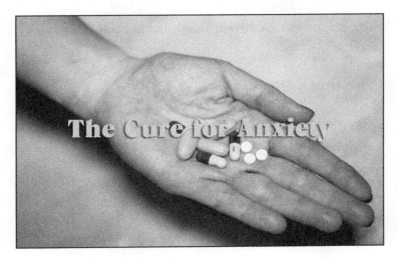

Scan Me!

Definition of anxious: afraid or nervous especially about what may happen.

There is a 50/50 chance of the outcome, if it happens not, then fine!

If it happens then deal with it!

> Rev. 21:8 But the fearful, and unbelieving, and the abominable, and murderers, and whoremongers, and sorcerers, and idolaters, and all liars, shall have their part in the lake which burneth with fire and brimstone: which is the second death.

Being fearful shows NO faith in God!

Listen to what Paul and Jesus taught as the cure for anxiety!

> Php 4:6 Be careful (ANXIOUS) for nothing; but in everything by prayer and supplication with thanksgiving let your requests be made known unto God.

> Php 4:7 And the peace of God, which passeth all understanding, shall keep your hearts and minds through Christ Jesus.

Did you know that the word "CAREFUL" above comes from the Greek word below?

μεριμνάω
Merimnaō
mer-im-nah'-o

From G3308; to be anxious about: - (be, have) care (-ful), take thought.

> Mat 6:25　Therefore I say unto you, Take no thought for your life, what ye shall eat, or what ye shall drink; nor yet for your body, what ye shall put on. Is not the life more than meat, and the body than raiment?

> Mat 6:26　Behold the fowls of the air: for they sow not, neither do they reap, nor gather into barns; yet your heavenly Father feedeth them. Are ye not much better than they?

> Mat 6:27　Which of you by taking thought can add one cubit unto his stature?
> Mat 6:28　And why take ye thought for raiment? Consider the lilies of the field, how they grow; they toil not, neither do they spin:

> Mat 6:29　And yet I say unto you, That even Solomon in all his glory was not arrayed like one of these.

Mat 6:30 Wherefore, if God so clothe the grass of the field, which to day is, and to morrow is cast into the oven, shall he not much more clothe you, O ye of little faith?

Mat 6:31 Therefore take no thought, saying, What shall we eat? or, What shall we drink? or, Wherewithal shall we be clothed?

Mat 6:32 (For after all these things do the Gentiles seek:) for your heavenly Father knoweth that ye have need of all these things.

Mat 6:33 But seek ye first the kingdom of God, and his righteousness; and all these things shall be added unto you.

Mat 6:34 Take therefore no thought for the morrow: for the morrow shall take thought for the things of itself. Sufficient unto the day is the evil thereof.

Luk 12:22 And he said unto his disciples, Therefore I say unto you, Take no thought for your life, what ye shall eat; neither for the body, what ye shall put on.

Luk 12:23 The life is more than meat, and the body is more than raiment.

Luk 12:24 Consider the ravens: for they neither sow nor reap; which neither have storehouse nor barn; and God feedeth them: how much more are ye better than the fowls?

Luk 12:25 And which of you with taking thought can add to his stature one cubit?

Luk 12:26 If ye then be not able to do that thing which is least, why take ye thought for the rest?

Luk 12:27 Consider the lilies how they grow: they toil not, they spin not; and yet I say unto you, that Solomon in all his glory was not arrayed like one of these.

Luk 12:28 If then God so clothe the grass, which is to day in the field, and to morrow is cast into the oven; how much more will he clothe you, O ye of little faith?

Luk 12:29 And seek not ye what ye shall eat, or what ye shall drink, neither be ye of doubtful mind.

Luk 12:30 For all these things do the nations of the world seek after: and your Father knoweth that ye have need of these things.

Luk 12:31 But rather seek ye the kingdom of God; and all these things shall be added unto you.

A spiritual voyage into the pages of the Bible

Luk 12:32   Fear not, little flock; for it is your
Father's good pleasure to give you the kingdom.

Ages and Dispensations

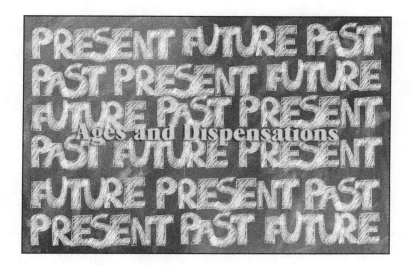

Scan Me!

There are 5 "AGES" taught in the Bible.

Paul mentions a few, I have listed them below.

> Eph_2:7 That in the ages to come he might shew the exceeding riches of his grace in his kindness toward us through Christ Jesus.

> Eph_3:5 Which in other ages was not made known unto the sons of men, as it is now revealed unto his holy apostles and prophets by the Spirit;

> Eph_3:21 Unto him be glory in the church by Christ Jesus throughout all ages, world without end. Amen.

> Col_1:26 Even the mystery which hath been hid from ages and from generations, but now is made manifest to his saints:

There is also the Past Ages, what God did in the eternal past before Gen. 1:1 is not revealed, but we know that he drafted His plan in that time. Ps .90:2; Prov. 8:22

1. The Ante-chaotic age Gen. 1:1 – Gen. 1:2
2. The Ante-diluvian age Gen. 1:3 – Gen. 6-8
3. The Present age Gen. 6-8 – Rev. 19:11-20:7
4. The Age to come Rev. 19:11-21 – Rev. 21-22
5. The Age of Ages, Eternity, time without end.

There are also 9 "DISPENSATIONS" in the Bible. The first was the Dispensation of Angels Isa.14:12-14; Ezek. 28:11-17; Col. 1:16-18 This dispensation took place long before the 6 days of Genesis, and Adam and Eve.

The world calls this dispensation the age of the dinosaurs.

Once again Paul taught this.

> 1Co_9:17 For if I do this thing willingly, I have a reward: but if against my will, a dispensation of the gospel is committed unto me.

> Eph_1:10 That in the dispensation of the fulness of times he might gather together in one all things in Christ, both which are in heaven, and which are on earth; even in him:

> Eph_3:2 If ye have heard of the dispensation of the grace of God which is given me to you-ward:

> Col_1:25 Whereof I am made a minister, according to the dispensation of God which is given to me for you, to fulfil the word of God;

Then there are 7 dispensations with Man.

1. Dispensation of innocence
   Gen. 1:26-3:24
   From creation of Adam and Eve until their fall from grace.

2. Dispensation of conscience
   Gen. 4:1-8:14
   From the fall of Adam and Eve to Noah's flood.

3. Dispensation of human government
   Gen. 8:15-11:9
   From after Noah's flood to the Call of Abraham.

4. Dispensation of promise
   Gen. 11:10 - Ex. 12:51
   From the call of Abraham to the Exodus of the children of Israel from Egypt.

5. Dispensation of law
   Ex. 13:1 - Matt. 4:1; 11:10-13; Lk. 16:16
   From after the Exodus to the preaching of John the Baptist.

6. Dispensation of grace
   Matt. 4:1 - Rev. 19:21
   From the first Advent of Jesus Christ to His Second Advent.

7. Dispensation of Divine government
   Rev. 20:1-15
   From the Second Advent of Jesus Christ to the end of the Millennium.

The last will be the Dispensation of the Redeemed and faithful Angels.
   Rev. 21:1-22:5; 1 Cor. 15:24-28

From after the end of the Millennium and unto eternity.

This is rightly dividing the Word of God.

> 2 Tim. 2:15 Study to shew thyself approved unto God, a workman that needeth not to be ashamed, rightly dividing the word of truth.

If we erred God is gracious enough to forgive us, it is but because of our pride that we sometimes hold on to non-scriptural doctrines. We are commanded to test all doctrine, to see if it comes from God or the Deceiver.

> 1 Thes. 5:21 Prove all things; hold fast that which is good.

The Bible clearly teaches about dispensations!

Dispensation, or Administration are periods of time that start with God's dealing with men in favorable circumstances, with a particular test, and end in failure and judgment.

What God said during one dispensation may or may not be applied to another.

This will help answer a lot of your questions. Right now I suggest you focus on getting to know God in the New Testament. For all that is written in the New Testament applies to us living right now, in this the present dispensation of Grace.

1. **Dispensation of Innocence:** From the creation of Adam and Eve who were created sinless, to when they sinned and were expulsed from the Garden of Eden. Did not last long I would give it less than a week!

2. **Dispensation of Conscience:** From the expulsion from the Garden of Eden to the flood of Noah. Lasted 1,656 years.

3. **Dispensation of Human Government:** From the flood of Noah, to the call of Abraham. Lasted 427 years.

4. **Dispensation of Promise:** From the call of Abraham, to the exodus of Israel from Egypt. Lasted 430 years.

5. **Dispensation of Law:** From the exodus of Israel from Egypt, to the preaching of John the Baptist, or from Moses, to Jesus' first coming. Lasted a little over 1,700 years.

6. **Dispensation of Grace:** From Jesus' first coming, to Jesus' second coming. Lasted so far over 2000 years.

7. **Dispensation of Divine Government – The Millennium:** This age will start when Jesus comes back to set up the Kingdom of Heaven on Earth: It will

last 1,000 years.

8. **Dispensation of the Redeemed and faithful Angels:** After the 1,000 years, all sin will be purged, and God will then move His capital from the planet Heaven, to the planet Earth. The Kingdom of Heaven, will give way to the Kingdom of God!

After reading that twice, you should now understand that God deals with groups of people in different ways.

We hope this helps you understand that converting to Judaism is going backwards and is not according to God's plan.

A spiritual voyage into the pages of the Bible

Use this space for notes

The End of Days

Scan Me!

The end of days is not now!

I will give you 1 verse to remember!

> Dan 9:27 And he shall confirm the covenant with many for one week: and in the midst of the week he shall cause the sacrifice and the oblation to cease, and for the overspreading of abominations he shall make it desolate, even until the consummation, and that determined shall be poured upon the desolate.

So any monkey out there predicting the end of days without this verse in mind is totally blind!

For the countdown to start, the Jewish people have to make a 7-year peace covenant with the Antichrist and start sacrificing animals, and as of today, not 1 animal has been sacrificed!

It might happen in 7 years or in another 7,000 years! Only God the Father knows!

Now to the Jews the 9th of Av is a day of fasting and prayer; the destruction of both their first and second temple took place on that day.

In their eyes they blame the Goyim, yet they should look deeper inside themselves and see that it was because of their continued resistance to the Holy Ghost, and their continual practice of idolatry that was the cause of the destruction of both their temples.

They are slow learners and will rejoice for a while with yet another temple in Israel, which Christ will destroy and finally build the 4th and final Temple.

The majority of the Jewish people will not get converted until they finally see Christ Jesus with their own eyes. Thank God that there will be 144,000 that will see the light and be rewarded with living in the Gated Community with the Creators and Saviors of the human race.

So the next time the 9th of Av comes by, tell a Jewish friend to stop crying and fasting, and be glad that God will finally give them their Holy Temple in Israel, but that will only happen after Christ's Second Advent and NOT before!

This way you have revealed the Truth to them, and perhaps they will want to hear more good news.

Remember that all have sinned, including Jewish people, we are not here to judge but to point to Christ Jesus, their Messiah our Christ and both our Savior.

A spiritual voyage into the pages of the Bible

Use this space for notes

Chapter 5
Truth & Fairy Tales

If you want the truth then read the Bible, if you prefer fairy tales, then I recommend the Talmud.

The Bible is God inspired and points to Christ.

The Talmud is not God inspired and points away from Christ.

The Bible does not burden us with rules and regulations, yet the Talmud is packed with rules and regulations; what you can eat, what you can wear, how much can you walk on the Sabbath day and so on.

Seriously, if that was the case, then what is this freedom Paul talked about?

> Rom_8:2 For the law of the Spirit of life in Christ Jesus hath made me free from the law of sin and death.

Why You Should Use The King James Bible

Because it is nearly perfect in it's translation from both the original Hebrew and Greek texts.

The only *error* I found was the use of the word "Easter" which should have been translated as in all other places as Passover.

Other versions are OK for now, as long as you are reading them, but for serious study do invest in a King James Bible.

You can search online and see the actual reasons why you should use the King James Version. I don't want to start problems, but rest assured this is the version you should use.

Math in the Bible & Proof of Contact With Aliens

On page 16 of this book, I briefly touched on the subject of some ambitious projects that a group of notable and highly respected scientists embarked upon, regarding communicating with extraterrestrials in outer space.

After many years of study and research, these scientists concluded that an advanced alien civilization would attempt to contact other sentient beings, using a universal language called mathematics!

We don't have to venture far to see practical applications of using math to communicate with non-human species. Right here on this earth zoologists have uncovered that certain animals have the ability to count and recognize simple geometric shapes.

On this premise, we can see that mathematics is universally known as a tool to determine the source of *objective truth*.

Music can also be considered in the same way. Each note or tone has a unique pitch and frequency that is easily recognizable as sound with patterns. We can also apply this logic to shapes and geometry. A triangle will always have 3 sides, a square 4, and so on. Numbers and letters change with cultures, times and places. Basic geometric shapes will never change no matter where you are in the universe.

For example, to represent the number 3, we can use the following shapes seen in Figure 1:

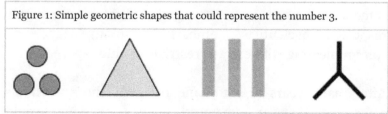

Figure 1: Simple geometric shapes that could represent the number 3.

The book you are reading now is using an alphabet system that evolved over hundreds to thousands of years.

For example, the letter A is similar in many languages around the world and is usually denoted by the first letter of the alphabet.   Hence in Greek alpha, and aleph in Hebrew, mean prime or the first.

For our numbers 0 - 9, they too have evolved over time. We inherited this system from India sometime in the 6th century.

There are some cases however where numerals and letters can be substituted.

We have all heard of, seen or used Roman numerals at some time or the other. I = 1, V=5, X=10, L = 50 and so on.

Well, it's a little-known fact that both Hebrew and Greek, the language that the Old and New Testaments were written in, use the same letters in their alphabet to express written numbers, as seen in Table 2 and Table 3.

Table 2 - Hebrew alphanumeric characters and values

No	Symbol	Name	Numerical Value
1	א	Aleph	1
2	ב	Beth	2
3	ג	Gimel	3
4	ד	Daleth	4
5	ה	He	5
6	ו	Vav	6
7	ז	Zayin	7
8	ח	Het	8
9	ט	Tet	9

A spiritual voyage into the pages of the Bible

Table 2 - continued ..

No	Symbol	Name	Numerical Value
10	י	Yod	10
11	כ	Kaf	20
12	ל	Lamed	30
13	מ	Mem	40
14	נ	Nun	50
15	ס	Samekh	60
16	ע	Ayin	70
17	פ	Pe	80
18	צ	Tsadi	90
19	ק	Qoph	100
20	ר	Resh	200
21	ש	Shin	300
22	ת	Tav	400
23	ך	Kaf	500
24	ם	Final Mem	600
25	ן	Final Nun	700
26	ף	Final Pe	800
27	ץ	Final Tsadi	900

Table 3 - Greek alphanumeric characters and values

No	Symbol	Name	Numerical Value
1	A α	Alpha	1
2	B β	Beta	2
3	Γ γ	Gamma	3

A spiritual voyage into the pages of the Bible

Table 3 - continued ..

No	Symbol	Name	Numerical Value
4	Δ δ	Delta	4
5	E ε	Epsilon	5
6	ς′	Diagamma	6
7	Z ζ	Zeta	7
8	H η	Eta	8
9	Θ θ	Theta	9
10	I ι	Iota	10
11	K κ	Kappa	20
12	Λ λ	Lambda	30
13	M μ	Mu	40
14	N ν	Nu	50
15	Ξ ξ	Xi	60
16	O o	Omicron	70
17	Π π	Pi	80
18	ϟ	Koppa	90
19	P ρ	Rho	100
20	Σ σ	Sigma	200
21	T τ	Tau	300
22	Y υ	Upsilon	400
23	Φ φ	Phi	500
24	X χ	Chi	600
25	Ψ ψ	Psi	700
26	Ω ω	Omega	800
27	ϡ	Sampi	900

In both Hebrew and Greek, not only does each letter represent a value, but each word contains the sum of all its letters added up.

For now, our focus will be on the Hebrew content of Genesis 1:1. The number seen on top of each grouping of words is the sum of its individual characters. Hebrew is read from right to left.

The first thing we notice is that there are 7 words totaling **28** characters in total, where **4 x 7 = 28**.

We can also see that there are 3 main nouns, *"God"*, *"heaven"* and *"earth"*. Their numeric values in Hebrew are 86 + 395+ 296, which total **777**, or **111 x 7**!

The first verb in Genesis 1:1, *"created"* has a value of **203**, or **29 x 7**.

The first 3 Hebrew words "In the beginning - created - God" has **14** letters, or **2 x 7**.

The last 4 Hebrew words " את - *the heaven - and - the earth*" also have **14** letters, or **2 x 7**.

Remember, this is only the *first verse* of the Bible.

The Bible is full of references using the number 7 or multiples of 7 in both the Old and New Testaments. Here are just a few of many hundreds!

- 7 days of creation of (Gen 1)
- 7th day of rest (Gen 2:2-3)
- The Feast of Unleavened Bread lasts 7 days (Exo 12,13)
- The Feast of Tabernacles in the 7th month lasting 7 days (Lev. 23:34)
- God gave Moses 70 helpers (Num 11:24-25)
- 14,700 dead (Num 16:49)
- 7 priests, 7 trumpets, 7 marches, 7th day (Jos 6:4)
- 7 pipes, 7 lamps of (Zec 4:2)
- 7 stars, 7 churches, 7 candlesticks (Rev 1:20)
- 7 seals (Rev 6:1), 7 trumpets (Rev 8:6), 7 bowls (Rev 16:1)

On that note, we present you the reader with the following challenge!

We invite you to come up with **your own list of 7 words** and **try to repeat the patterns we uncovered here in**

Genesis 1:1. You can use any words you like, and those 7 words can be about anything you want.

Then you can take the challenge to the next level, by writing a book about the story of your family and how the reader is an integral part of that story. It must contain 66 books, with 39 chapters written in your native language, and the other 27 chapters are written in a foreign language, by someone you will never meet, separated by over 1,000 years of time, and from a land and culture vastly different from yours, and their version of facts must agree with yours!

If you can do that, with or without a computer then you can duplicate what we find in the Bible. You're a genius and should be awarded a Nobel Prize of some sort!

Until then, no other book or written piece of literature from the entire history of humanity has (or can) come close to reproducing this incredible feat! We feel it's a safe bet no one will, unless they can predict all future events with 100% accuracy!

We invite you to search the scriptures for yourself and discover what other numerical patterns exist, and there are many! Not just with the number 7, but with 3, 8, 10, 12, 40, and in many complex forms that would keep the mathematician and scientist in you busy for weeks and months for sure!

The whole point of this exercise is to show that the way that the pages, chapters, and events are arranged and recorded in the Bible can by no means have been done by any one person, or group of people regardless of how brilliant or simple-minded they were.

There are too many independent factors to consider that make it very unlikely that the books of the Bible were haphazardly strung together.

What this shows is that without a doubt, a higher intelligence than man was responsible for its authoring, editing, and distribution.

When people say they were inspired by the Holy Spirit, well, this is the perfect example. These miraculous feats are the "footprints" and "digital signature" of the Holy Spirit and how He works through mankind to accomplish the will of God the Father.

Without the aid of high-speed computers, it would not be possible to analyze the intricate details found in the mathematics that binds each letter, word, and phrase of God's story about us, and for us and why us.

So, where's the part about proof of contact with Aliens?

> Exo 18:3 And her two sons; of which the name of the one was Gershom; for he said, I have been an **alien** in a strange land:

Deu 14:21 Ye shall not eat of any thing that dieth of itself: thou shalt give it unto the stranger that is in thy gates, that he may eat it; or thou mayest sell it unto an **alien**: for thou art an holy people unto the LORD thy God. Thou shalt not seethe a kid in his mother's milk.

Job 19:15 They that dwell in mine house, and my maids, count me for a stranger: I am an **alien** in their sight.

Psa 69:8 I am become a stranger unto my brethren, and an **alien** unto my mother's children.

Isa 61:5 And strangers shall stand and feed your flocks, and the sons of the **alien** shall be your plowmen and your vinedressers.

And finally, the proof that life exists elsewhere outside of planet Earth;

Joh 18:36 **Jesus answered,** My kingdom is not of this world: if my kingdom were of this world, then would my servants fight, that I should not be delivered to the Jews: but now is my kingdom not from hence.

I, for one look forward to the day where I will be "abducted" by the Aliens (Elohim/אלהים), and taken to their home planet (Heaven), to serve them for all eternity!

---

1 Th 4:17 Then we which are alive and remain shall be caught up together with them in the clouds, to meet the Lord in the air: and so shall we ever be with the Lord.

So, instead of spending billions of dollars on using radio telescopes pointed to the stars to look and listen for a message from an alien civilization thousands of light years away, pick up a copy of the King James Version of the Bible and simply believe everything you read in it!

It will cost much less, and you won't have to wait for thousands of years to get a reply! Aliens love to communicate with math, music and geometry. If you want to reach out to them, play some music, sing a hymn. They also love company, so why not invite some friends over to add to the experience! You get bonus points for referrals.

I sincerely think it's time we rethink who and what aliens are. They are not what Hollywood and the media portray in movies and on TV, nor are they figments of the imagination of people that some mental health experts would call bipolar or detached from reality.

If you ask me, you'd have to be crazy not to believe in aliens after reading this book and understanding what the Bible is really all about.

You never know, an alien might save your life one day ...

A spiritual voyage into the pages of the Bible

Use this space for notes

What Is Everything Made Of?

Scan Me!

Mat 5:14 Ye are the light of the world. A city that is set on an hill cannot be hid.

Psa 82:6 I have said, Ye are gods; and all of you are children of the most High.

Note: To help you better understand the information and the context in this part of the book, we invite you to read our 5-part series called *"What is everything made of?"* by scanning the *QR code* on the bottom of the previous page with your smartphone or tablet.

Once you've done that, here's a little recap of what we've discovered so far:

In **Part I** of this series, we were introduced to the scale of the universe, from the very large to the very small.

In **Part II**, we discovered what the limits are at the smallest scale of the universe, and essentially what makes up the stuff inside and all around us.

In **Part III**, we demonstrated how the world, everything inside of us and everything that surrounds us is made up of light (physical and localized) and information (non-physical and non-local).

These days there is a lot of talk coming from highly respected scientists that they believe our world is a hologram or computer simulation. Their reasons for believing this come from many scientific experiments that were performed, and the mathematical equations that were used to form their theories.

What these people and many others like them have in common is that they understand there is more to our reality than meets the eye, albeit from a secular perspective. They understand that our physical nature is more than just flesh and bones, but is chiefly made of light, and can be altered genetically or by directly interfacing with machine technology. Within the next 20 or so years, a new breed of humans will walk the face of the earth!

Today we can see the early stages of this new humanity. Consider how times have changed since the turn of the 1900's. Since the time that Christ Jesus last walked the earth among us, humanity was generally "quiet" for about 2,000 years. Then at the turn of the 1900s, our way of life drastically changed thanks to the industrial revolution.

But what does this all mean for you, the average person? Why should you care about what science has to say about what's out there and what will happen to humanity within the next 20 years? Why should you care about what the Bible says? Does it really make a difference in your life if any of this matters to you? Will any of this make any kind of an impact on your day to day living?

Well, let's take a look at how we live today compared to about 150 years ago. On July 1st, 1867, the country of Canada (my home and native land) was born. My home town of Montreal this year is celebrating the 375th anniversary of its founding by representatives of the Catholic Church on May 17, 1642.

This is relatively young for a country, compared to the "old world" which has been around for hundreds to thousands of years. Like Egypt, China and some isolated cultures living in jungles and ocean islands scattered around the world that have yet to be discovered by modern society.

The way people "did things day to day" hadn't really changed much from the time the first explorers came to the eastern shores of Canada in 1534, until its founding as a country in 1867.

Prior to the turn of the 20th century, the rate of change of technology was very slow. Hundreds of years would pass before major advances were made and became commonplace amongst the population. When compared with how we live today, every 18 months we come up with a new breakthrough in some area of science or the other, and the pace is still accelerating!

Technology has improved, knowledge has increased BUT ... has any of this helped humanity to live peacefully with each other?

Despite all the good that technology has brought us to improve the quality of our lives, moral values are in free fall. Despite the fact that there are enough material resources available for everyone on this planet to live comfortably, we still struggle with poverty, excessive greed, incurable diseases, violent crimes, escalating global conflicts between nations, dishonest and corrupt politics, dysfunctional families, gender identity issues, and many other societal ills that we once thought technology and the enlightened human spirit would eliminate.

If technology can't save us, then who or what can?

Well, the Bible is very clear about the answer to this question. Problem is, the society we live in today rejects anything that has to do with living a godly life, or that a higher power is in charge of human affairs in this world.

You might be asking why is the Bible so special out of all the books that have ever existed? What does Judaism or Christianity have that's so special over Islam, Hinduism, Buddhism, or any of the hundreds of "peaceful" religions or ways of life that people choose to live by?

One of the greatest scientific discoveries of our time was made by a Russian mathematician named Ivan Panin.

At the turn of the 20th century, he discovered a hidden code written within the pages of the Bible that no person could have produced or duplicated on their own, with or without the aid of a machine. No other piece of literature ever written self-authenticates itself, including all works from religious texts worldwide. His discovery is as important to humanity as the one made by Jean-François Champollion in 1822, the French scholar who was the first to completely decipher and translate the Egyptian hieroglyphics, with the aid of the Rosetta Stone, his gift for languages and a curious mind.

The Bible is what it is, and what it says is the only truth there is that tells the story of where we came from, why we are here and what our destiny will be for all eternity.

This life is like a game, and the Bible explains how to play to win, and the consequences of when you play to lose. Some people don't like to play by the rules, but if we look at the structure of what makes everything in our universe, we clearly see that there is an order to how things work. Without this order, there would be chaos, and nothing would be able to exist as we know it!

Life is about balance. It is about learning to live in harmony with our environment. When we learn to be in harmony with ourselves, then everything else will fall into place!

Therefore, it doesn't really make any difference if our world is a simulation or not! What matters are the choices that we make each day, and if they are in harmony with God's laws. People make it a point to pay their rent or their taxes on time. They also respect the law of the land and would think twice about lying to the police or a judge.

This means that no one has any excuse (once they reach the age of reason, which is about 12 years old in all cultures), to not know the difference between right and wrong. All people, all countries, everyone past, present and future is subject to God's laws which cannot be annulled or repealed! There are no exceptions, not even in death!

The reason this is so important and vital to understanding is that YOU ARE A CREATED BEING! You were not put here by accident, It does not matter what happened to you in the past, or where you happen to be in life today. Rich or poor, healthy or sick, young or old, famous or reclusive.

Did you know that you are a god in training!! You were created for a purpose and there is a plan for your life here on this earth!

You were created to replace a workforce that mutinied against the Godhead. They are the ⅓ of angels with Lucifer/Satan that rebelled against God. They were fired from their jobs managing the affairs of this planet and the universe, evicted from their homes, and they know that humans are taking their places.

As you can imagine, they're not too happy about it and will do everything in their power to torment and discourage humanity from finding out the truth about their destiny. This explains why there are so many conspiracies and cover-ups on so many subjects. It's to keep the global population dumbed down and unable to think for themselves to discover the truth.

But rest assured! Once you discover it, you have Divine protection! So long as you do your part as a Christian, the Godhead will do their part to secure your peace of mind and well-being in a mixed-up world, until the time comes for them to take you to your inheritance in Heaven, for all eternity! Your reward for believing in them, at all costs!

> Joh 1:3 All things were made by him; and without him was not any thing made that was made.

> Col 1: 15-17 For by him were all things created, that are in heaven, and that are in earth, visible and invisible, whether they be thrones, or dominions, or principalities, or powers: all things were created by him, and for him: And he is before all things, and by him all things consist.

> 1 Pet 2:9 But ye are a chosen generation, a royal priesthood, an holy nation, a peculiar people; that ye should shew forth the praises of him who hath called you out of darkness into his marvellous light;

If you've never read the Bible or don't understand science too well, don't worry, you're not alone! In fact, many of us take science and the Bible for granted or believe that both can't be right, so they choose one over the other. Usually, it's science over the Bible.

In the past 100 years, the human race has reached unprecedented advances in science and technology. Ultimately, this has allowed us to understand what we and the rest of the universe are made of and why we are here.

Why is this important to understand?

At some point in your life, you will experience some form of a personal tragedy. The death of a loved one. Being forced to flee your home country for safety from persecution. Losing your job. Going through a divorce. Being diagnosed with a terminal illness. Losing everything you spent your whole life working for.

Whatever it may be, no matter how much you try to protect and prepare yourself, hard times will come, and usually when you least expect it.

When these tragedies strike, it usually leaves the person feeling vulnerable, shaken and looking for answers. Some find comfort in substance abuse, depression, or get involved with risky behavior that could put that person's life or the people around them in danger.

These attitudes are usually associated with people who feel lost, lonely with nobody to turn to for help. Some people end their lives on their own, thinking their pain and suffering will be over.

Well, before we go any further, let's make a few things clear about the subject of death. In this reality that we all live in, there is no such thing as being "dead", where "you" as a person totally stop existing and are permanently incapable of being conscious of anything ever again. What we call "death" today is what the Bible calls a "temporary state of existence". No soul sleep is taught! Only the body sleeps in the ground.

Everyone that has died will come back to life and spend eternity in a physical body in one of two places; the restored earth and heaven or the lake of fire.

The restored earth and heaven will be the home for all those who ever lived that made an effort to change their lives for the better and kept their word through good and bad. Even if they died trying, as long as they believed in Jesus Christ, some way, some how, they will get a second chance at a better life.

If you are reading this today, and you are a "born again" Christian, there is the very real possibility that by the close of this current "generation", you will not experience death as you know it. Instead, you will be transformed into a new person with a new body that will never get sick or die from natural causes!

This is to prepare you for your new role as part of God's team of government administrators and other civil service roles that will require you to have enhanced body functions to eventually work in space and on other planetary systems.

> Rev 1:6 And hath made us kings and priests unto God and his Father; to him be glory and dominion for ever and ever. Amen

Now then, if you know that you stand a chance to be exempt from dying a physical death, by getting sick or from an accident, and you know you're guaranteed a comprehensive benefits plan in God's Kingdom on Earth there should no longer be any reason to allow fear or stress to control your life!

Without Jesus in your life, you live in constant fear because you have no way to allow your mind to get rid of the stress that causes your body to wear itself down.

This is the reason why people eventually get sick and eventually die; lack of faith or belief! They end up doing themselves in, by living life in constant fear and uncertainty. They never know if they'll have enough of whatever it is they think they need to get by, make their ends meet and feel happy in life.

Instead of allowing God to have control over the affairs of their lives, they take matters into their own hands, trading one set of worries for another, and it never ends, till the day they end up getting sick and dying. There is no shortage of worries that do nothing but reduce the years and quality of life from good people.

Living by faith is not as hard as you think. It may take a little while to get used to, but once you start seeing the positive changes in your life, you will never want to go back to living the way you did before! Not too many people catch on to the "not dying" part, but once you do, you can begin to rebuild your life with greater purpose!

You think this idea sounds crazy? Does the idea of not dying sound like an impossible dream?

Well, let's first look at some important facts that will give you something to think about. Then you can decide for yourself whether it's time you changed your mind and habits about life and death.

The science that says we are immortal and can live forever, comes from the same science that is used to create medicines that save lives, send people to the moon and back, genetically modify the food that you eat, keep track of your financial affairs, create the technology that you depend upon for survival every day, and so many other things that we take for granted each day.

Scientists today can essentially *clone* (make a copy of) a human being and record its thoughts onto a computer, so it can see on a computer screen images and video of what he sees through its eyes or through its thoughts and dreams. Viruses, diseases, cancer, depression, Alzheimer's, you name it. Any disease of the body or mind can be "cured" with a software program uploaded to your brain! No more pills, surgery or therapy required!

I want you to think about that for a minute. If you have enough money, you'll be able to pay a clinic to fix you up for good! The problem is, this would be a health care system for the rich and powerful. The average person would never be able to afford it unless they inherited a lot of money or won the lottery.

The idea of humans being immortal is nothing new. The Bible is very clear on the subject of immortality. God is immortal, and so are you, simply because you and I were made in his image. Immortality is in our genes! God did not use technology to become what he is.

He simply believed in himself and in the other members that make up the Holy Trinity, to do their part in their great and wonderful plan for the universe, our home and your part in it!

That's right! You were created to be like your creator! You were created to live a peaceful life, with no stress, and to be prosperous and happy. This was the life that Adam and Eve once had. The struggles and hardships we all face, including working to death is part of the curse we all inherited when Adam and Eve disobeyed God's plan for survival in his world.

You wouldn't play a game without first learning the rules, or how it's played. You wouldn't take apart an engine or change a part on your car without first consulting some kind of manual.

It's the same with your body, life, and the Bible. You were made with care and are designed to function in perfect harmony with your environment. You can't drive a car for long without putting in gas. When driven for a long time, oil, brakes, tires, filters and spark plugs need to be changed, otherwise, the car will not drive well and will wear down much sooner than needed.

In this world, to get the best out of your body and life, you need to read the Bible and learn to live a faith-based life. It is the only way to find and keep true freedom and happiness!

Now, you must make a choice! Continue to live and depend on human science and ingenuity or the Bible and living by faith as a born-again Christian.

Of course, you are free to do your own research, and spend years of your life looking for the answers to living a better life. You can find out the hard way that leaving the Bible out of your life is like committing spiritual suicide, or you can put your pride aside, pick up a King James Version of the Bible and begin reading for yourself.

You can start by reading the first chapter of the Book of John in the New Testament or the first chapter of the Book of Revelation, and get your free blessing!

> Rev 1:3 Blessed is he that readeth, and they that hear the words of this prophecy and keep those things that are written therein: for the time is at hand.

Hell Unleashed!

Coming soon!

Hollywood teaches about aliens invading from outer space, but the Bible teaches that aliens will invade and torment men from under the Earth!

That's right, these aliens are coming up from Hell, and not down from outer space!

Unlike the movies where mankind kills them off in the last 3 minutes of the movie, mankind will be helpless against these aliens, since they are spirit beings and cannot be killed by humans!

Rev 9:1 And the fifth angel sounded, and I saw a star fall from heaven unto the earth: and to him was given the key of the bottomless pit.

Rev 9:2 And he opened the bottomless pit; and there arose a smoke out of the pit, as the smoke of a great furnace; and the sun and the air were darkened by reason of the smoke of the pit.

Rev 9:3 And there came out of the smoke locusts upon the earth: and unto them was given power, as the scorpions of the earth have power.

Rev 9:4 And it was commanded them that they should not hurt the grass of the earth, neither any green thing, neither any tree; but only those men which have not the seal of God in their foreheads.

Rev 9:5 And to them it was given that they should not kill them, but that they should be tormented five months: and their torment was as the torment of a scorpion, when he striketh a man.

Rev 9:6 And in those days shall men seek death, and shall not find it; and shall desire to die, and death shall flee from them.

Rev 9:7   And the shapes of the locusts were like unto horses prepared unto battle; and on their heads were as it were crowns like gold, and their faces were as the faces of men.

Rev 9:8   And they had hair as the hair of women, and their teeth were as the teeth of lions.

Rev 9:9   And they had breastplates, as it were breastplates of iron; and the sound of their wings was as the sound of chariots of many horses running to battle.

Rev 9:10   And they had tails like unto scorpions, and there were stings in their tails: and their power was to hurt men five months.

Rev 9:11   And they had a king over them, which is the angel of the bottomless pit, whose name in the Hebrew tongue is Abaddon, but in the Greek tongue hath his name Apollyon.

Men will seek to die in those days, but the law of death will be put on hold for 5 months!

Will bring a whole new meaning to "He/She suffered before he/she died!"

Once again these are literal beings!

They have;

1. Bodies like horses

2. Heads like men

3. Crowns of gold

4. Hair like women

5. Teeth like lions

6. Breastplates of iron

7. Wings

8. Tails and scorpion stings

Once again you can save yourself from being a cast member of the movie by accepting Jesus Christ as your personal Savior today, so when the movie comes out, you can watch it in the safety of the Heavenly theater!

The truth about the 200,000,000 demon horsemen from Hell!

Rev 9:12 One woe is past; *and,* behold, there come two woes more hereafter.

Rev 9:13 And the sixth angel sounded, and I heard a voice from the four horns of the golden altar which is before God,

Rev 9:14 Saying to the sixth angel which had the trumpet, Loose the four angels which are bound in the great river Euphrates.

Rev 9:15 And the four angels were loosed, which were prepared for an hour, and a day, and a month, and a year, for to slay the third part of men.

Rev 9:16 And the number of the army of the horsemen *were* two hundred thousand thousand: and I heard the number of them.

Rev 9:17 And thus I saw the horses in the vision, and them that sat on them, having breastplates of fire, and of jacinth, and brimstone: and the heads of the horses *were* as the heads of lions; and out of their mouths issued fire and smoke and brimstone.

Rev 9:18 By these three was the third part of men killed, by the fire, and by the smoke, and by the brimstone, which issued out of their mouths.

Rev 9:19 For their power is in their mouth, and in their tails: for their tails *were* like unto serpents, and had heads, and with them they do hurt.

Rev 9:20 And the rest of the men which were not killed by these plagues yet repented not of the works of their hands, that they should not worship devils, and idols of gold, and silver, and brass, and stone, and of wood: which neither can see, nor hear, nor walk:

Rev 9:21 Neither repented they of their murders, nor of their sorceries, nor of their fornication, nor of their thefts.

The 4 angels bound in the Euphrates are fallen ones. **Faithful angels are never bound!**

They are leaders of the 200,000,000 demon horsemen who are now bound in the Abyss and will be loosed under the 6th trumpet to cause the second woe announced by the angel.

Mankind will not be able to protect themselves, nor be able to kill them, for they are spirit beings and thus man is the weaker of the two!

They will slay 1/3 of mankind in 1 hour (60 minutes) at a certain year, month, and day!

How will these 1/3 sinners perish you ask?

Well there are 3 ways listed!

1. By the fire of their mouths

2. By the smoke of their mouths

3. By the brimstone out of their mouths

The men that are not killed by these plagues will only harden themselves against God and continue in demon and idol worship, you know like Pharaoh of old!

So to be on the safe side, destroy your idols before they are the cause of your destruction!

The truth about a fallen angel called in the Hebrew tongue Abaddon, and in the Greek Apollyon

Most people who have read the entire Bible first came to the knowledge of this fallen angelic being in the last book of the New Testament.

But he was first mentioned in the first book of the Bible ever written, and to tell the truth, the book of Job was the first one written, even before Moses wrote his 5 books. Well once again when Moses wrote his books, they were originally all in 1 book. His book got split up later on, but back to Abaddon!

Below is the verse most people will quote when Abaddon is mentioned!

> Rev 9:11 And they had a king over them, *which is* the angel of the bottomless pit, whose name in the Hebrew tongue *is* Abaddon, but in the Greek tongue hath *his* name Apollyon.

Now John was Jewish, and had read all of the Old Testament, so where did he get this name from? Well below I have listed a few sources, starting with Job!

You will quickly notice that the word Abaddon is nowhere to be found in the verses below, but rest assured he is clearly there in the Hebrew text!

In all the verses below when you see the word "destruction" in the original Hebrew it is plainly written Abaddon.

> Job 26:6 Hell *is* naked before him, and destruction (Abaddon) hath no covering.

> Job 28:22 Destruction (Abaddon) and death say, We have heard the fame thereof with our ears.

Notice: Death is also considered to be a *fallen angel*!

> Job 31:12 For it *is* a fire *that* consumeth to destruction (Abaddon), and would root out all mine increase.

> Psa 88:11 Shall thy lovingkindness be declared in the grave? *or* thy faithfulness in destruction (Abaddon)?

> Pro 15:11   Hell and destruction (Abaddon) *are* before the LORD: how much more then the hearts of the children of men?

> Pro 27:20   Hell and destruction (Abaddon) are never full; so the eyes of man are never satisfied.

So from reading the verses above you will notice that Hell is not Abaddon, in fact Abaddon is a fallen angel who is a king of an army of **200,000,000 demon horsemen**, who are locked up in the deepest compartment of Hell which is known as the Abyss. No lost human soul has ever been seen that far down!

If you made up your mind on believing everything written in the Bible, then believe that Abaddon is a real fallen angel, and if you don't believe, I guarantee that when he comes out you will believe!

The benefit of believing now is that you won't be around when he finally shows up! You will be in Heaven watching all that is happening down here on Earth.

A spiritual voyage into the pages of the Bible

Use this space for notes

What Happens When We Die?

Death Defined

The word death in the Bible can be substituted with the word separation!

It <u>never</u> means annihilation!

The Bible teaches 2 kinds of deaths.

1. Physical death is the separation of the inner man (soul and spirit) from the outer man (human body).

2. Spiritual death is the separation of man (body, soul, and spirit) from God due to sin.

Both saved souls **and** sinners **WILL LIVE FOREVER** in peace and comfort or eternal punishment!

The choice is left up to you to make!

There will be no one to blame in the end but yourself if you reject God's free gift of Salvation through Christ Jesus.

The only difference is that the saved soul will never be separated from God again. As for the separated sinner; he will face the second death, which means eternal separation from God in the Lake of fire!

Did you know that souls of men wear clothes after death?

BTW, there will not be colorful clothes in Heaven. White is the color du jour, and yes it will be Kosher to wear white after labor day!

Moses wore clothes when he appeared with Christ.

> Mat 17:1 And after six days Jesus taketh Peter, James, and John his brother, and bringeth them up into an high mountain apart,

Mat 17:2 And was transfigured before them: and his face did shine as the sun, and his raiment was white as the light.

Mat 17:3 And, behold, there appeared unto them Moses and Elias talking with him.

Since Elijah did not die (yet) I did not mention him above with Moses! He was taken to Heaven in a chariot!

2 Kin 2:1 And it came to pass, when the LORD would take up Elijah into heaven by a whirlwind, that Elijah went with Elisha from Gilgal.

2 Kin 2:9 And it came to pass, when they were gone over, that Elijah said unto Elisha, Ask what I shall do for thee, before I be taken away from thee. And Elisha said, I pray thee, let a double portion of thy spirit be upon me.

2 Kin 2:10 And he said, Thou hast asked a hard thing: nevertheless, if thou see me when I am taken from thee, it shall be so unto thee; but if not, it shall not be so.

2 Kin 2:11 And it came to pass, as they still went on, and talked, that, behold, there appeared a chariot of fire, and horses of fire, and parted them both asunder; and Elijah went up by a whirlwind into heaven.

2 Kin 2:12 And Elisha saw it, and he cried, My father, my father, the chariot of Israel, and the horsemen thereof. And he saw him no more: and he took hold of his own clothes, and rent them in two pieces.

2 Kin 2:14 He took up also the mantle of Elijah that fell from him, and went back, and stood by the bank of Jordan;

Enoch is the only other human that did not experience a physical death (yet) because God took him to Heaven for being an upright person.

Gen 5:21 And Enoch lived sixty and five years, and begat Methuselah:

Gen 5:22 And Enoch walked with God after he begat Methuselah three hundred years, and begat sons and daughters:

Gen 5:23 And all the days of Enoch were three hundred sixty and five years:

Gen 5:24 And Enoch walked with God: and he was not; for God took him.

The souls under the altar were given clothes to put on.

Rev 6:9 And when he had opened the fifth seal, I saw under the altar the souls of them that were slain for the word of God, and for the testimony which they held:

Rev 6:10 And they cried with a loud voice, saying, How long, O Lord, holy and true, dost thou not judge and avenge our blood on them that dwell on the earth?

Rev 6:11 And white robes were given unto every one of them; and it was said unto them, that they should rest yet for a little season, until their fellowservants also and their brethren, that should be killed as they were, should be fulfilled.

So souls of men have substance, it is called a spirit body, an exact Xerox copy of the human body they had while alive on earth.

Souls separated from their bodies can also see, feel, and communicate to other souls.

Luk 16:22 And it came to pass, that the beggar died, and was carried by the angels into Abraham's bosom: the rich man also died, and was buried;

Luk 16:23 And in hell he lift up his eyes, being in torments, and seeth Abraham afar off, and Lazarus in his bosom.

Luk 16:24 And he cried and said, Father Abraham, have mercy on me, and send Lazarus, that he may dip the tip of his finger in water, and cool my tongue; for I am tormented in this flame.

Luk 16:25 But Abraham said, Son, remember that thou in thy lifetime receivedst thy good things, and likewise Lazarus evil things: but now he is comforted, and thou art tormented.

Luk 16:26 And beside all this, between us and you there is a great gulf fixed: so that they which would pass from hence to you cannot; neither can they pass to us, that would come from thence.

Departed souls can also be rejoined with their separated bodies and live again!

1 Ki 17:17 And it came to pass after these things, that the son of the woman, the mistress of the house, fell sick; and his sickness was so sore, that there was no breath left in him.

1 Ki 17:18 And she said unto Elijah, What have I to do with thee, O thou man of God? art thou come unto me to call my sin to remembrance, and to slay my son?

1 Ki 17:19 And he said unto her, Give me thy son. And he took him out of her bosom, and carried him up into a loft, where he abode, and laid him upon his own bed.

1 Ki 17:21 And he stretched himself upon the child three times, and cried unto the LORD, and said, O LORD my God, I pray thee, let this child's soul come into him again.

1 Ki 17:22 And the LORD heard the voice of Elijah; and the soul of the child came into him again, and he revived.

And of course, one of the many miracles that Jesus performed. One time for Lazarus;

Joh 11:11 These things said he: and after that he saith unto them, Our friend Lazarus sleepeth; but I go, that I may awake him out of sleep.

Joh 11:17 Then when Jesus came, he found that he had lain in the grave four days already.

Joh 11:21 Then said Martha unto Jesus, Lord, if thou hadst been here, my brother had not died.

Joh 11:23 Jesus saith unto her, Thy brother shall rise again.

Joh 11:24 Martha saith unto him, I know that he shall rise again in the resurrection at the last day.

Joh 11:25 **Jesus said unto her,** I am the resurrection, and the life: he that believeth in me, though he were dead, yet shall he live:

Joh 11:41 Then they took away the stone from the place where the dead was laid. And Jesus lifted up his eyes, and said, Father, I thank thee that thou hast heard me.

Joh 11:42 And I knew that thou hearest me always: but because of the people which stand by I said it, that they may believe that thou hast sent me.

Joh 11:43 And when he thus had spoken, he cried with a loud voice, Lazarus, come forth.

Joh 11:44 And he that was dead came forth, bound hand and foot with graveclothes: and his face was bound about with a napkin. Jesus saith unto them, Loose him, and let him go

And another time for Jairus' daughter;

Luk 8:49 While he yet spake, there cometh one from the ruler of the synagogue's house, saying to him, Thy daughter is dead; trouble not the Master.

Luk 8:50 But when Jesus heard it, he answered him, saying, Fear not: believe only, and she shall be made whole.

Luk 8:52 And all wept, and bewailed her: but he said, Weep not; she is not dead, but sleepeth.

Luk 8:53 And they laughed him to scorn, knowing that she was dead.

Luk 8:54 And he put them all out, and took her by the hand, and called, saying, Maid, arise.

Luk 8:55 And her spirit came again, and she arose straightway: and he commanded to give her meat.

Rev 1:18 I am he that liveth, and was dead; and, behold, I am alive for evermore, Amen; and have the keys of hell and of death.

The whole point of these Biblical messages is that if there is no resurrection, then there is no point in preaching the Gospel!

1 Cor 15:12 Now if Christ be preached that he rose from the dead, how say some among you that there is no resurrection of the dead?

1 Cor 15:13 But if there be no resurrection of the dead, then is Christ not risen:

1 Cor 15:14 And if Christ be not risen, then is our preaching vain, and your faith is also vain.

There is talk these days from the scientific community that they have evidence that there is an afterlife, and that a person still has awareness of where they are after their body has died (legally brain dead).

1Co_1:18 For the preaching of the cross is to them that perish foolishness; but unto us which are saved it is the power of God.

1Co_1:21 For after that in the wisdom of God the world by wisdom knew not God, it pleased God by the foolishness of preaching to save them that believe.

1Co_1:23 But we preach Christ crucified, unto the Jews a stumblingblock, and unto the Greeks foolishness;

1Co_1:25 Because the foolishness of God is wiser than men; and the weakness of God is stronger than men.

1Co_2:14 But the natural man receiveth not the things of the Spirit of God: for they are foolishness unto him: neither can he know them, because they are spiritually discerned.

1Co_3:19 For the wisdom of this world is foolishness with God. For it is written, He taketh the wise in their own craftiness.

For the Biblically minded person, here is what the scientific and medical communities are only now beginning to understand. Once a person has an "awareness", it stays on forever! When their body dies, their minds remain active and they are aware of their surroundings. This means that that the mind can exist without a physical body (similar to what we all experience while dreaming)!

Note: People that have *out-of-body experiences*, or can have *lucid dreams* will have an idea of what it feels like to experience reality without the use of a physical body. Paul speaks about such an experience here:

2 Cor 12:13 And I knew such a man, (whether in the body, or out of the body, I cannot tell: God knoweth;)

2 Cor 12:14 How that he was caught up into paradise, and heard unspeakable words, which it is not lawful for a man to utter.

The two verses above teach us that under certain circumstances, a person can have an out-of-body experience, and can visit the *paradise* section of heaven!

Psa 13:3 Consider and hear me, O Lord my God: lighten mine eyes, lest I sleep the sleep of death;

Dan 12:2 And many of them that sleep in the dust of the earth shall awake, some to everlasting life, and some to shame and everlasting contempt.

The end of death and dying!

1 Cor 15:51 Behold, I shew you a mystery; We shall not all sleep, but we shall all be changed,

1 Cor 15:52 In a moment, in the twinkling of an eye, at the last trump: for the trumpet shall sound, and the dead shall be raised incorruptible, and we shall be changed.

1 Cor 15:53 For this corruptible must put on incorruption, and this mortal must put on immortality.

1 Cor 15:54 So when this corruptible shall have put on incorruption, and this mortal shall have put on immortality, then shall be brought to pass the saying that is written, Death is swallowed up in victory.

1 Cor 15:55 O death, where is thy sting? O grave, where is thy victory?

1 Cor 15:56 The sting of death is sin; and the strength of sin is the law. But thanks be to God, which giveth us the victory through our Lord Jesus Christ.

Gen 2:7 And the LORD God formed man of the dust of the ground, and breathed into his nostrils the breath of life; and man became a living soul.

Notice that God formed man out of the dust. Till this stage man was just a body, the second part is the kicker!

God breathed into his nostrils *"The Breath of Life"* the final result was Man became a *"living soul!"*

How do people die and why?

Sin and lack of faith separate a person from God. When a person sins and does not repent, they disqualify themselves from God's universal healthcare plan, and substitute it with their own, thus taking any chances that come along with it.

When this person dies, a physical death takes place separating the living soul from its body. The body is the only part that goes back to dust, as for the living soul; well you know there are 2 possible places for that living soul to go to!

Each human being has 3 parts:

- a body (the visible part) The only part that sleeps and goes back to dust.
- a soul (the part that God breathed life into, invisible to us) the part that feels and gives him self-consciousness.

- a spirit (the person's life experiences and character, also invisible to us) the part that knows and makes him self-determined and a free moral agent.

According to scripture, **your body is a vessel**, like a ship or a car! It is the part that moves through physical space.

Your soul is the part of God that gives your body the energy to become a living person behind the wheel. This is the part that God breathes (life) into each human being. Your spirit is your accumulated driving and life experiences that help you safely navigate the roads and oceans of life.

Rom_9:21 Hath not the potter power over the clay, of the same lump to make one vessel unto honour, and another unto dishonour?

1Th_4:4 That every one of you should know how to possess his vessel in sanctification and honour;

2Ti_2:21 If a man therefore purge himself from these, he shall be a vessel unto honour, sanctified, and meet for the master's use, and prepared unto every good work.

1Pe_3:7 Likewise, ye husbands, dwell with them according to knowledge, giving honour unto the wife, as unto the weaker vessel, and as being heirs together of the grace of life; that your prayers be not hindered.

G4632

σκεῦος

skeuos

skyoo'-os

Of uncertain affinity; a vessel, implement, equipment or apparatus (literally or figuratively [specifically a wife as contributing to the usefulness of the husband]): - goods, sail, stuff, vessel.

Now each of us as Captain of our vessel, is solely responsible for our crew (the trillions of cells that make up body)!

If you cannot command your vessel according to what High Command has established as Moral rules, and if you give into rebellion like your crew then you will be destroyed along with your crew.

Christ was the First man to have a perfect crew, and thanks to His guide book for Captains you too with proper training can have that same crew!

It's only 1 crew member to add to your vessel, and His name is the Holy Spirit!

So, what will it be ... Heaven or Hell?

You choose this day where you want your soul to go at death!

Use this space for notes

I Identify as LGBTQ

As you are reading this part of the book, I hope to show you something different. Not necessarily new, but different. If you're familiar with the LGBTQ community, then you already know the importance of diversity. It challenges us to explore our humanity, and exchange ideas with others in ways that weren't possible before.

The experiment I would like for you to try can be done from anywhere. At home, at work, on the train or bus ride home ... time and place do not matter. All you need to do is trust what you see and hopefully, you'll understand what I'm trying to point out to you.

I want you to go look at yourself in a mirror. If you don't have a mirror, use your phone to look at yourself, or you can take a selfie.

Take a good look. What do you see?

The very first thing you should notice is a complex living organism called a human being. At this point, we're not looking at the age, gender, or social status of this human being, we are simply observing (and perhaps admiring) who they are. The human body is a remarkable living organism. Given the right conditions, it can accomplish amazing things. Given the wrong conditions, it can accomplish terrible things too.

Look at yourself again in the mirror. What more do you see?

If you looked at the news lately, there's a whole lot of hate and intolerance going in places where hate shouldn't be anymore.

When these people go home and look themselves in the mirror, what do you think they see? Most likely, they probably see the same thing as you. A human being, a person, looking a certain way ... a face with details, and that would be pretty much it.

At the end of the day, this person in the mirror will go to bed with thoughts of how they spent their past day, maybe have some thoughts about plans for the next day and beyond ... and then perhaps drift off and think about things from their past.

If we sum things up right there, we can clearly see that when we look in the mirror, we see a living organism, called a human being, that has a certain shape, size, and colour, and has the ability to change the way they feel (emotions), based on certain conditions or circumstances.

Ultimately, we are a collection of cells experiencing moments in time. Whether the experience occurred in the past, or is happening now, or is yet to come, every single cell within us goes through and feels the same experiences as the whole body, and stores that information in the DNA, memory cells in the brain, heart and stomach.

Now, did you know that there's a science at work that keeps that image of yourself alive?   Unless you've been living under a rock, scientists today have discovered some very interesting things about our bodies.   For one, they've discovered that ultimately, we are holographic in nature and that given the right conditions, our physical nature can live on for eternity! So then, what keeps us from living forever? Well, it's the "S" word.

Stress. You thought I was going to say "sin", but alas, not this time my dear friends!

Yes, stress kills. Without going into a long speech about the whole process, stress is the reason why cells in your body break down with age, to the point where they can no longer function and reproduce perfectly as they were originally designed to do. Since stress originates from the mind not being able to cope with a given situation presented to it (cognitive dissonance), we can conclude that our thoughts and the ability to manage them can make or break us.

For the most part, people spend the majority of their time stressing about survival. Not just keeping up with bills and making sure food is on the table, but worrying about health, sexuality, future plans and many other things that most of us cram our minds with day in and day out, without ever considering what those thoughts are doing to our bodies.

This goes on for years. Decades even. Then to make things worse, most people worry about their retirement or funeral plans. Who gets what when they die, what's to be done with property and assets, etc ... and of course the money problem is thrown in for good measure.

Then one day, they end up looking themselves in a mirror, see a total mess, and wonder to themselves how did things ever get this way ... and eventually, struggle for a solution to these compounding problems. More stress.

And then they die, someday ... but guaranteed, any happiness they had in their life while they were alive is mostly a fleeting memory and gone by the time they're on their deathbed, usually in some kind of pain before they go off to never-never land.

Then the cycle repeats. Every person who ever lived goes through this experience.

And that's the official story ... that the establishment wants you to believe. You're born, you live out an existence for a time, and then bye bye, you're gone. Boring huh? Kind of sad if you ask me. But, wouldn't you know it, there's an alternative way to live! It costs nothing more than your time and ability to understand things for yourself. A small investment for a very large payout! ... but, are you ready and prepared to accept the challenge?

Okay, so now that you got used to looking at yourself in a mirror if you have a partner in a committed relationship, both of you stand in the mirror and look at yourselves.

What do you see?

If you followed along correctly, you should see not one, but two unique living organisms called human beings.

Not only can these human beings interact with themselves, but they can do it between each other using a variety of ways to communicate. Touch, speech, nonverbal, just to name a few.

While you're both looking at each other in the mirror, I would like to present a couple of truths to you. From there, you'll need to do some deductive reasoning and some homework on your own. Nothing complicated, but very simple and it's common sense.

Truth #1: The world around you is something like a hologram. If you're not sure what that means, quite simply it means that everything around you is made and organized in such a way, that it would be as if you are living your life inside of a video game. If you watched movies like The Matrix, you can assume that the world you live in is a programmed reality. Everything happens for a reason. There are no such things as coincidences, as ALL events are predestined to occur (more on this another time)!

Truth #2: Your body is a hologram. If you're not sure what that means, think of it this way: you can modify your body not only by thoughts but also with technology. You are like a digital character in a video game. Created by a programmer ... a designer, and are therefore predictable in EVERY manner known to him! DNA is the microscopic software code that makes you what you are via genetic and environmental factors.

If you can accept these two truths, then you should be able to understand the concept of upgrades or improvements to the original programming of the user in the game.

Now if life can be compared to a game or a programmed reality, then there must be something that explains how the rules of the game are played. Fortunately, we have such a rule book, and it's called The Bible.

The 66 books of the King James Version, the version used to make all other translations worldwide, was written and structured in such a way that cannot be replicated, duplicated or forged by any process known to humans today!

Since the world around us can be reduced to "code" (i.e. biological life via DNA, all forms of matter such as liquids, solids, gases and plasma via chemical bonds), we can conclude that there is a structure and order to the world around us and within us. Nothing is by accident!

Just like with any machine, it usually comes with an instruction and maintenance manual so that the machinery can operate to its fullest capacity, and if things break down, how and where to get the repair.

Look in the mirror again. It's getting very important now!

Just like most software programs or computing machines (including smartphones) that we know, they can be upgraded or patched with apps and such. Well, it's the same thing with our bodies! The human machine, regardless of age, gender and race is designed to be upgraded! That upgrade includes the ability to:

- be exempt from sickness and death
- have regenerative and shape shifting abilities
- break the limitations of the speed of light
- manipulate objects by thoughts
- walk through solid objects
- eat and drink without gaining weight
- and much more

Quite impressive isn't it. What's the catch? You have to follow the rules it says you must live by in order to be eligible for the upgrade once it becomes available.

What rules? Well, as from what I can gather, there is but ONE important rule to follow:

> Mat 19:21 **Jesus said unto him,** If thou wilt be perfect, go and sell that thou hast, and give to the poor, and thou shalt have treasure in heaven: and come and follow me.

As a human being, contemplating this article and that one Bible quote you've just read, ask yourself: Is it worth it to keep living with stress and problems and eventually get sick, die and be buried OR, take the chance to follow what Jesus said so that you can get your reward and treasure in Heaven AND get to enjoy dual citizenship between Heaven and Earth, with a new body that will never get sick or perish, and live out many wonderful and amazing adventures that no person alive on earth today or anytime in the future could ever promise you.

All you have to do is follow Jesus and put Him FIRST in everything that you do. That's it, that's all. If you can do that honestly and truthfully, Jesus will send the Holy Spirit to guide you through your new adventures in life as a new creature with benefits that are literally out of this world!

If you are in a long-term or committed relationship, looking in the mirror with your partner after reading through all this, and fact checking things to see that indeed the truth is being told here, ask yourself this very important question:

> *The person that is sitting or standing next to you looking in that mirror. Would you stand in their way of getting a system upgrade to their body that would cure them of all sickness and disease and let them live in peace and harmony for all eternity?*

I'm going to ask this again differently;

> *If you truly love the person you're partnered with, would you temporarily give up everything you own as a sacrifice to follow Jesus, so that you can get back everything you lost plus interest?*

Look in the mirror again, what do you see? Look at your partner again, what do you see? Do you both still see things the same way, or a little different somehow?

We are going to follow up with this at a later date. But first, please take the time to think about what you just read, and how it applies to you. How you answer will determine if you are a friend or foe to humanity, so stay tuned!

A spiritual voyage into the pages of the Bible

Use this space for notes

A Tale of Two Planets: Heaven and Earth

Did you know that the Bible plainly states that the Earth is round? The term "four corners" means the 4 directions! Isaiah plainly said "circle".

> Isa 40:22 It is he that sitteth upon the circle of the earth, and the inhabitants thereof are as grasshoppers; that stretcheth out the heavens as a curtain, and spreadeth them out as a tent to dwell in:

Isa 11:12   And he shall set up an ensign for the nations, and shall assemble the outcasts of Israel, and gather together the dispersed of Judah from the four corners of the earth.

Mat 24:31   And he shall send his angels with a great sound of a trumpet, and they shall gather together his elect from the four winds, from one end of heaven to the other.

Rev 7:1   And after these things I saw four angels standing on the four corners of the earth, holding the four winds of the earth, that the wind should not blow on the earth, nor on the sea, nor on any tree.

North is always upwards.
South is always downwards.
East is always rightwards.
West is always leftwards.

The Bible also states that Heaven is northward!

So now, what about Heaven? What does it look like? Does it have a size and shape? Is it some kind of infinite expanse somewhere in another dimension? Does it have white fluffy clouds, pearly gates and Saint Peter patiently waiting to welcome new members and give them their harps?

Believe it or not, Heaven is a real place. In fact it is a planet, not so much different from the earth we are on now!

How do we know this for a fact?

Well, from the very start, in Genesis 1:1 it is clearly stated that the Elohim created the heaven and the earth.

He made them to be inhabited.

> Isa 45:18 For thus saith the LORD that created the heavens; God himself that formed the earth and made it; he hath established it, he created it not in vain, he formed it to be inhabited: I am the LORD; and there is none else.

Ultimately, earth will be "terraformed" to be an identical but smaller copy of heaven!

> Mat 6:10 Thy kingdom come. Thy will be done in earth, as it is in heaven.

This verse teaches us that gradually over time, planet Earth will become more like planet Heaven!

Most people have read how Enoch and Elijah were translated and taken to Heaven, but did you know there were other instances in the Bible where some people were able to visit planet Heaven for a short time?

If we read Zechariah chapters 4, 5 and 6, we see that the Old Testament prophet was in an altered state and was taken on a trip with an angel where he sees many strange things that he is unfamiliar with. Namely candlesticks, lamps, olive trees, bowls, horses, chariots, mountains of brass and scrolls.

> Zec 4:1 And the angel that talked with me came again, and waked me, as a man that is wakened out of his sleep.

Now, if we compare what Zechariah saw with what John saw in his revelation from Jesus, we see many of the same symbols!

We also see that John was in an altered state when he saw his visions.

> Rev 1:9 I John, who also am your brother, and companion in tribulation, and in the kingdom and patience of Jesus Christ, was in the isle that is called Patmos, for the word of God, and for the testimony of Jesus Christ.

> Rev 1:10 I was in the Spirit on the Lord's day, and heard behind me a great voice, as of a trumpet,

Rev 1:11 Saying, I am Alpha and Omega, the first and the last: and, What thou seest, write in a book, and send it unto the seven churches which are in Asia; unto Ephesus, and unto Smyrna, and unto Pergamos, and unto Thyatira, and unto Sardis, and unto Philadelphia, and unto Laodicea.

Rev 1:12 And I turned to see the voice that spake with me. And being turned, I saw seven golden candlesticks;

From these verses, we clearly see that John was in Heaven when he saw these things.

Then there is the apostle Paul's experience;

2 Cor 12:1 It is not expedient for me doubtless to glory. I will come to visions and revelations of the Lord.

2 Cor 12:2 I knew a man in Christ above fourteen years ago, (whether in the body, I cannot tell; or whether out of the body, I cannot tell: God knoweth;) such an one caught up to the third heaven.

2 Cor 12:3 And I knew such a man, (whether in the body, or out of the body, I cannot tell: God knoweth;)

> 2 Cor 12: 4 How that he was caught up into paradise, and heard unspeakable words, which it is not lawful for a man to utter.

Now that we see that Heaven is accessible to people under special conditions, where is it located?

The old testament reveals to us some hints as to its location;

> Isa 14:12 How art thou fallen from heaven, O Lucifer, son of the morning! how art thou cut down to the ground, which didst weaken the nations!

> Isa 14:13 For thou hast said in thine heart, I will ascend into heaven, I will exalt my throne above the stars of God: I will sit also upon the mount of the congregation, in the sides of the north:

The above verses teach us that the planet Heaven is in the northern part of our skies, relative to earth in space.

The following verse teaches us that it has an orbit in space;

> Job 22:14 Thick clouds are a covering to him, that he seeth not; and he walketh in the circuit of heaven.

And that it has an orbit within that space;

Psa 19:6 His going forth is from the end of the heaven, and his circuit unto the ends of it: and there is nothing hid from the heat thereof.

The main difference between heaven and earth is that the inhabitants of earth are spiritually blind! As a result, they have corrupted and enslaved the people on this planet. This was the result of Lucifer's influence on Adam and Eve, and consequently every person who has ever lived since then, with the exception of Christ Jesus, who broke this curse.

This *blindness* prevents ordinary people from being capable of reasoning using spiritual guidance instead of human intuition. Our reasoning abilities are very limited, and although we as a species have achieved great things, our physical brains are limited in how they analyze, interpret and process information.

This is the reason why a born again Christian needs to pray for guidance from the Holy Spirit. Once a person gradually increases in spiritual strength, they will gain a better understanding of God's purpose for humanity. This will ultimately prepare them to be raptured and changed from this weak human body to a hybrid light-energy body that can do more and never get tired or old!

Only with this upgrade will the rest of the secrets of the universe, including how the Elohim (Gods) created everything in this universe out of nothing will finally be known and understood.

Use this space for notes

Chapter 6
A Collection of Psalms

What are Psalms?

When David instituted hymns in Israel, he appointed the Levites (priests) with very special instructions:

> 1 Chr 16:4 And he appointed certain of the Levites to minister before the ark of the Lord, and to record, and to thank and praise the LORD God of Israel:

The Psalms are a historical and cultural record of the Jews in Israel while David was king. They contain praises, thanksgivings and supplications to God by His people.

This has served to bring comfort, encouragement and blessings to God's people throughout all cultures and ages. Every known human emotion is expressed in the verses and chapters of the psalms, which were originally sung and set to music, all to the glory of the Gods.

Psalms of Praise

Psalms 8

To the chief Musician upon Gittith, A Psalm of David.

¹ O LORD our Lord, how excellent is thy name in all the earth! who hast set thy glory above the heavens.
² Out of the mouth of babes and sucklings hast thou ordained strength because of thine enemies, that thou mightest still the enemy and the avenger.
³ When I consider thy heavens, the work of thy fingers, the moon and the stars, which thou hast ordained;
⁴ What is man, that thou art mindful of him? and the son of man, that thou visitest him?
⁵ For thou hast made him a little lower than the angels, and hast crowned him with glory and honour.
⁶ Thou madest him to have dominion over the works of thy hands; thou hast put all things under his feet:
⁷ All sheep and oxen, yea, and the beasts of the field;
⁸ The fowl of the air, and the fish of the sea, and whatsoever passeth through the paths of the seas.
⁹ O LORD our Lord, how excellent is thy name in all the earth!

Psalms 33

¹ Rejoice in the LORD, O ye righteous: for praise is comely for the upright.

² Praise the LORD with harp: sing unto him with the psaltery and an instrument of ten strings.

³ Sing unto him a new song; play skilfully with a loud noise.

⁴ For the word of the LORD is right; and all his works are done in truth.

⁵ He loveth righteousness and judgment: the earth is full of the goodness of the LORD.

⁶ By the word of the LORD were the heavens made; and all the host of them by the breath of his mouth.

⁷ He gathereth the waters of the sea together as an heap: he layeth up the depth in storehouses.

⁸ Let all the earth fear the LORD: let all the inhabitants of the world stand in awe of him.

⁹ For he spake, and it was done; he commanded, and it stood fast.

¹⁰ The LORD bringeth the counsel of the heathen to nought: he maketh the devices of the people of none effect.

¹¹ The counsel of the LORD standeth for ever, the thoughts of his heart to all generations.

¹² Blessed is the nation whose God is the LORD; and the people whom he hath chosen for his own inheritance.

¹³ The LORD looketh from heaven; he beholdeth all the sons of men.

¹⁴ From the place of his habitation he looketh upon all the inhabitants of the earth.

¹⁵ He fashioneth their hearts alike; he considereth all their works.

¹⁶ There is no king saved by the multitude of an host: a mighty man is not delivered by much strength.

¹⁷ An horse is a vain thing for safety: neither shall he deliver any by his great strength.

¹⁸ Behold, the eye of the LORD is upon them that fear him, upon them that hope in his mercy;

¹⁹ To deliver their soul from death, and to keep them alive in famine.

²⁰ Our soul waiteth for the LORD: he is our help and our shield.

²¹ For our heart shall rejoice in him, because we have trusted in his holy name.

²² Let thy mercy, O LORD, be upon us, according as we hope in thee.

Psalms 111

¹ Praise ye the LORD. I will praise the LORD with my whole heart, in the assembly of the upright, and in the congregation.

² The works of the LORD are great, sought out of all them that have pleasure therein.

³ His work is honourable and glorious: and his righteousness endureth for ever.

⁴ He hath made his wonderful works to be remembered: the LORD is gracious and full of compassion.

⁵ He hath given meat unto them that fear him: he will ever be mindful of his covenant.

⁶ He hath shewed his people the power of his works, that he may give them the heritage of the heathen.

⁷ The works of his hands are verity and judgment; all his commandments are sure.

⁸ They stand fast for ever and ever, and are done in truth and uprightness.

⁹ He sent redemption unto his people: he hath commanded his covenant for ever: holy and reverend is his name.

¹⁰ The fear of the LORD is the beginning of wisdom: a good understanding have all they that do his commandments: his praise endureth for ever.

Psalms 135

¹ Praise ye the LORD. Praise ye the name of the LORD; praise him, O ye servants of the LORD.

² Ye that stand in the house of the LORD, in the courts of the house of our God,

³ Praise the LORD; for the LORD is good: sing praises unto his name; for it is pleasant.

⁴ For the LORD hath chosen Jacob unto himself, and Israel for his peculiar treasure.

⁵ For I know that the LORD is great, and that our Lord is above all gods.

⁶ Whatsoever the LORD pleased, that did he in heaven, and in earth, in the seas, and all deep places.

⁷ He causeth the vapours to ascend from the ends of the earth; he maketh lightnings for the rain; he bringeth the wind out of his treasuries.

⁸ Who smote the firstborn of Egypt, both of man and beast.

A spiritual voyage into the pages of the Bible

9 Who sent tokens and wonders into the midst of thee, O Egypt, upon Pharaoh, and upon all his servants.

10 Who smote great nations, and slew mighty kings;

11 Sihon king of the Amorites, and Og king of Bashan, and all the kingdoms of Canaan:

12 And gave their land for an heritage, an heritage unto Israel his people.

13 Thy name, O LORD, endureth for ever; and thy memorial, O LORD, throughout all generations.

14 For the LORD will judge his people, and he will repent himself concerning his servants.

15 The idols of the heathen are silver and gold, the work of men's hands.

16 They have mouths, but they speak not; eyes have they, but they see not;

17 They have ears, but they hear not; neither is there any breath in their mouths.

18 They that make them are like unto them: so is every one that trusteth in them.

19 Bless the LORD, O house of Israel: bless the LORD, O house of Aaron:

20 Bless the LORD, O house of Levi: ye that fear the LORD, bless the LORD.

21 Blessed be the LORD out of Zion, which dwelleth at Jerusalem. Praise ye the LORD.

Psalms of Thanksgiving

Psalm 9

To the chief Musician upon Muthlabben, A Psalm of David.

[1] I will praise thee, O LORD, with my whole heart; I will shew forth all thy marvellous works.

[2] I will be glad and rejoice in thee: I will sing praise to thy name, O thou most High.

[3] When mine enemies are turned back, they shall fall and perish at thy presence.

[4] For thou hast maintained my right and my cause; thou satest in the throne judging right.

[5] Thou hast rebuked the heathen, thou hast destroyed the wicked, thou hast put out their name for ever and ever.

[6] O thou enemy, destructions are come to a perpetual end: and thou hast destroyed cities; their memorial is perished with them.

[7] But the LORD shall endure for ever: he hath prepared his throne for judgment.

[8] And he shall judge the world in righteousness, he shall minister judgment to the people in uprightness.

[9] The LORD also will be a refuge for the oppressed, a refuge in times of trouble.

[10] And they that know thy name will put their trust in thee: for thou, LORD, hast not forsaken them that seek thee.

[11] Sing praises to the LORD, which dwelleth in Zion: declare among the people his doings.

[12] When he maketh inquisition for blood, he remembereth them: he forgetteth not the cry of the humble.

[13] Have mercy upon me, O LORD; consider my trouble which I suffer of them that hate me, thou that liftest me up from the gates of death:

[14] That I may shew forth all thy praise in the gates of the daughter of Zion: I will rejoice in thy salvation.

[15] The heathen are sunk down in the pit that they made: in the net which they hid is their own foot taken.

[16] The LORD is known by the judgment which he executeth: the wicked is snared in the work of his own hands. Higgaion. Selah.

[17] The wicked shall be turned into hell, and all the nations that forget God.

[18] For the needy shall not alway be forgotten: the expectation of the poor shall not perish for ever.

[19] Arise, O LORD; let not man prevail: let the heathen be judged in thy sight.

[20] Put them in fear, O LORD: that the nations may know themselves to be but men. Selah.

Psalm 10

[1] Why standest thou afar off, O LORD? why hidest thou thyself in times of trouble?

[2] The wicked in his pride doth persecute the poor: let them be taken in the devices that they have imagined.

[3] For the wicked boasteth of his heart's desire, and blesseth the covetous, whom the LORD abhorreth.

[4] The wicked, through the pride of his countenance, will not seek after God: God is not in all his thoughts.

⁵ His ways are always grievous; thy judgments are far above out of his sight: as for all his enemies, he puffeth at them.

⁶ He hath said in his heart, I shall not be moved: for I shall never be in adversity.

⁷ His mouth is full of cursing and deceit and fraud: under his tongue is mischief and vanity.

⁸ He sitteth in the lurking places of the villages: in the secret places doth he murder the innocent: his eyes are privily set against the poor.

⁹ He lieth in wait secretly as a lion in his den: he lieth in wait to catch the poor: he doth catch the poor, when he draweth him into his net.

¹⁰ He croucheth, and humbleth himself, that the poor may fall by his strong ones.

¹¹ He hath said in his heart, God hath forgotten: he hideth his face; he will never see it.

¹² Arise, O LORD; O God, lift up thine hand: forget not the humble.

¹³ Wherefore doth the wicked contemn God? he hath said in his heart, Thou wilt not require it.

¹⁴ Thou hast seen it; for thou beholdest mischief and spite, to requite it with thy hand: the poor committeth himself unto thee; thou art the helper of the fatherless.

¹⁵ Break thou the arm of the wicked and the evil man: seek out his wickedness till thou find none.

¹⁶ The LORD is King for ever and ever: the heathen are perished out of his land.

¹⁷ LORD, thou hast heard the desire of the humble: thou wilt prepare their heart, thou wilt cause thine ear to hear:

¹⁸ To judge the fatherless and the oppressed, that the man of the earth may no more oppress.

Psalm 30

A Psalm and Song at the dedication of the house of David.

¹ I will extol thee, O LORD; for thou hast lifted me up, and hast not made my foes to rejoice over me.
² O LORD my God, I cried unto thee, and thou hast healed me.
³ O LORD, thou hast brought up my soul from the grave: thou hast kept me alive, that I should not go down to the pit.
⁴ Sing unto the LORD, O ye saints of his, and give thanks at the remembrance of his holiness.
⁵ For his anger endureth but a moment; in his favour is life: weeping may endure for a night, but joy cometh in the morning.
⁶ And in my prosperity I said, I shall never be moved.
⁷ LORD, by thy favour thou hast made my mountain to stand strong: thou didst hide thy face, and I was troubled.
⁸ I cried to thee, O LORD; and unto the LORD I made supplication.
⁹ What profit is there in my blood, when I go down to the pit? Shall the dust praise thee? shall it declare thy truth?
¹⁰ Hear, O LORD, and have mercy upon me: LORD, be thou my helper.

---

[11] Thou hast turned for me my mourning into dancing: thou hast put off my sackcloth, and girded me with gladness;
[12] To the end that my glory may sing praise to thee, and not be silent. O LORD my God, I will give thanks unto thee for ever.

Psalm 40

To the chief Musician, A Psalm of David.

[1] I waited patiently for the LORD; and he inclined unto me, and heard my cry.
[2] He brought me up also out of an horrible pit, out of the miry clay, and set my feet upon a rock, and established my goings.
[3] And he hath put a new song in my mouth, even praise unto our God: many shall see it, and fear, and shall trust in the LORD.
[4] Blessed is that man that maketh the LORD his trust, and respecteth not the proud, nor such as turn aside to lies.
[5] Many, O LORD my God, are thy wonderful works which thou hast done, and thy thoughts which are to us-ward: they cannot be reckoned up in order unto thee: if I would declare and speak of them, they are more than can be numbered.
[6] Sacrifice and offering thou didst not desire; mine ears hast thou opened: burnt offering and sin offering hast thou not required.

---

[7] Then said I, Lo, I come: in the volume of the book it is written of me,

[8] I delight to do thy will, O my God: yea, thy law is within my heart.

[9] I have preached righteousness in the great congregation: lo, I have not refrained my lips, O LORD, thou knowest.

[10] I have not hid thy righteousness within my heart; I have declared thy faithfulness and thy salvation: I have not concealed thy lovingkindness and thy truth from the great congregation.

[11] Withhold not thou thy tender mercies from me, O LORD: let thy lovingkindness and thy truth continually preserve me.

[12] For innumerable evils have compassed me about: mine iniquities have taken hold upon me, so that I am not able to look up; they are more than the hairs of mine head: therefore my heart faileth me.

[13] Be pleased, O LORD, to deliver me: O LORD, make haste to help me.

[14] Let them be ashamed and confounded together that seek after my soul to destroy it; let them be driven backward and put to shame that wish me evil.

[15] Let them be desolate for a reward of their shame that say unto me, Aha, aha.

[16] Let all those that seek thee rejoice and be glad in thee: let such as love thy salvation say continually, The LORD be magnified.

[17] But I am poor and needy; yet the Lord thinketh upon me: thou art my help and my deliverer; make no tarrying, O my God.

Psalms 116

¹ I love the LORD, because he hath heard my voice and my supplications.

² Because he hath inclined his ear unto me, therefore will I call upon him as long as I live.

³ The sorrows of death compassed me, and the pains of hell gat hold upon me: I found trouble and sorrow.

⁴ Then called I upon the name of the LORD; O LORD, I beseech thee, deliver my soul.

⁵ Gracious is the LORD, and righteous; yea, our God is merciful.

⁶ The LORD preserveth the simple: I was brought low, and he helped me.

⁷ Return unto thy rest, O my soul; for the LORD hath dealt bountifully with thee.

⁸ For thou hast delivered my soul from death, mine eyes from tears, and my feet from falling.

⁹ I will walk before the LORD in the land of the living.

¹⁰ I believed, therefore have I spoken: I was greatly afflicted:

¹¹ I said in my haste, All men are liars.

¹² What shall I render unto the LORD for all his benefits toward me?

¹³ I will take the cup of salvation, and call upon the name of the LORD.

¹⁴ I will pay my vows unto the LORD now in the presence of all his people.

¹⁵ Precious in the sight of the LORD is the death of his saints.

---

¹⁶ O LORD, truly I am thy servant; I am thy servant, and the son of thine handmaid: thou hast loosed my bonds.

¹⁷ I will offer to thee the sacrifice of thanksgiving, and will call upon the name of the LORD.

¹⁸ I will pay my vows unto the LORD now in the presence of all his people,

¹⁹ In the courts of the LORD's house, in the midst of thee, O Jerusalem. Praise ye the LORD.

Psalms To Get Closer to God

Psalms 23

A Psalm of David

[1] The LORD is my shepherd; I shall not want.

[2] He maketh me to lie down in green pastures: he leadeth me beside the still waters.

[3] He restoreth my soul: he leadeth me in the paths of righteousness for his name's sake.

[4] Yea, though I walk through the valley of the shadow of death, I will fear no evil: for thou art with me; thy rod and thy staff they comfort me.

[5] Thou preparest a table before me in the presence of mine enemies: thou anointest my head with oil; my cup runneth over.

[6] Surely goodness and mercy shall follow me all the days of my life: and I will dwell in the house of the LORD for ever.

Psalms 35

A Psalm of David.

¹ Plead my cause, O LORD, with them that strive with me: fight against them that fight against me.

² Take hold of shield and buckler, and stand up for mine help.

³ Draw out also the spear, and stop the way against them that persecute me: say unto my soul, I am thy salvation.

⁴ Let them be confounded and put to shame that seek after my soul: let them be turned back and brought to confusion that devise my hurt.

⁵ Let them be as chaff before the wind: and let the angel of the LORD chase them.

⁶ Let their way be dark and slippery: and let the angel of the LORD persecute them.*

⁷ For without cause have they hid for me their net in a pit, which without cause they have digged for my soul.

⁸ Let destruction come upon him at unawares; and let his net that he hath hid catch himself: into that very destruction let him fall.

⁹ And my soul shall be joyful in the LORD: it shall rejoice in his salvation.

¹⁰ All my bones shall say, LORD, who is like unto thee, which deliverest the poor from him that is too strong for him, yea, the poor and the needy from him that spoileth him?

¹¹ False witnesses did rise up; they laid to my charge things that I knew not.

---

¹² They rewarded me evil for good to the spoiling of my soul.

¹³ But as for me, when they were sick, my clothing was sackcloth: I humbled my soul with fasting; and my prayer returned into mine own bosom.

¹⁴ I behaved myself as though he had been my friend or brother: I bowed down heavily, as one that mourneth for his mother.

¹⁵ But in mine adversity they rejoiced, and gathered themselves together: yea, the abjects gathered themselves together against me, and I knew it not; they did tear me, and ceased not:

¹⁶ With hypocritical mockers in feasts, they gnashed upon me with their teeth.

¹⁷ Lord, how long wilt thou look on? rescue my soul from their destructions, my darling from the lions.

¹⁸ I will give thee thanks in the great congregation: I will praise thee among much people.

¹⁹ Let not them that are mine enemies wrongfully rejoice over me: neither let them wink with the eye that hate me without a cause.

²⁰ For they speak not peace: but they devise deceitful matters against them that are quiet in the land.

²¹ Yea, they opened their mouth wide against me, and said, Aha, aha, our eye hath seen it.

²² This thou hast seen, O LORD: keep not silence: O Lord, be not far from me.

²³ Stir up thyself, and awake to my judgment, even unto my cause, my God and my Lord.

²⁴ Judge me, O LORD my God, according to thy righteousness; and let them not rejoice over me.

---

²⁵ Let them not say in their hearts, Ah, so would we have it: let them not say, We have swallowed him up.

²⁶ Let them be ashamed and brought to confusion together that rejoice at mine hurt: let them be clothed with shame and dishonour that magnify themselves against me.

²⁷ Let them shout for joy, and be glad, that favour my righteous cause: yea, let them say continually, Let the LORD be magnified, which hath pleasure in the prosperity of his servant.

²⁸ And my tongue shall speak of thy righteousness and of thy praise all the day long.

Psalm 58

To the chief Musician, Al-taschith, Michtam of David.

¹ Do ye indeed speak righteousness, O congregation? do ye judge uprightly, O ye sons of men?

² Yea, in heart ye work wickedness; ye weigh the violence of your hands in the earth.

³ The wicked are estranged from the womb: they go astray as soon as they be born, speaking lies.‡

⁴ Their poison is like the poison of a serpent: they are like the deaf adder that stoppeth her ear;

⁵ Which will not hearken to the voice of charmers, charming never so wisely.

---

⁶ Break their teeth, O God, in their mouth: break out the great teeth of the young lions, O LORD.

⁷ Let them melt away as waters which run continually: when he bendeth his bow to shoot his arrows, let them be as cut in pieces.

⁸ As a snail which melteth, let every one of them pass away: like the untimely birth of a woman, that they may not see the sun.

⁹ Before your pots can feel the thorns, he shall take them away as with a whirlwind, both living, and in his wrath.

¹⁰ The righteous shall rejoice when he seeth the vengeance: he shall wash his feet in the blood of the wicked.

¹¹ So that a man shall say, Verily there is a reward for the righteous: verily he is a God that judgeth in the earth.

Psalm 83

A Song or Psalm of Asaph.

¹ Keep not thou silence, O God: hold not thy peace, and be not still, O God.

² For, lo, thine enemies make a tumult: and they that hate thee have lifted up the head.

³ They have taken crafty counsel against thy people, and consulted against thy hidden ones.

⁴ They have said, Come, and let us cut them off from being a nation; that the name of Israel may be no more in remembrance.

⁵ For they have consulted together with one consent: they are confederate against thee:

⁶ The tabernacles of Edom, and the Ishmaelites; of Moab, and the Hagarenes;

⁷ Gebal, and Ammon, and Amalek; the Philistines with the inhabitants of Tyre;

⁸ Assur also is joined with them: they have holpen the children of Lot. Selah.

⁹ Do unto them as unto the Midianites; as to Sisera, as to Jabin, at the brook of Kison:

¹⁰ Which perished at Endor: they became as dung for the earth.

¹¹ Make their nobles like Oreb, and like Zeeb: yea, all their princes as Zebah, and as Zalmunna:

¹² Who said, Let us take to ourselves the houses of God in possession.

¹³ O my God, make them like a wheel; as the stubble before the wind.

¹⁴ As the fire burneth a wood, and as the flame setteth the mountains on fire;

¹⁵ So persecute them with thy tempest, and make them afraid with thy storm.

¹⁶ Fill their faces with shame; that they may seek thy name, O LORD.

¹⁷ Let them be confounded and troubled for ever; yea, let them be put to shame, and perish:

¹⁸ That men may know that thou, whose name alone is JEHOVAH, art the most high over all the earth.

Chapter 7
A Few Hymns

A spiritual voyage into the pages of the Bible

He's My King

WORDS BY JAMES ROWE
MUSIC BY JAMES D. VAUGHAN

A spiritual voyage into the pages of the Bible

Jesus Paid it All

WORDS BY ELVINA M. HALL
MUSIC BY JOHN T. GRAPE

A spiritual voyage into the pages of the Bible

On Our Way Rejoicing

WORDS BY JOHN S. B. MONSELL (1811-1875)
MUSIC BY FRANZ JOSEF HAYDN (1782-1806)

A spiritual voyage into the pages of the Bible

Are You Washed In The Blood?

1. Have you been to Je - sus for the cleans - ing pow'r? Are you washed in the
2. Are you walk - ing dai - ly by the Sav - ior's side? Are you washed in the
3. When the Bride-groom com - eth will your robes be white, pure and white in the
4. Lay a - side the gar - ments that are stained with sin, And be washed in the

blood of the Lamb? Are you ful - ly trust - ing in His grace this hour? Are you
blood of the Lamb? Do you rest each mo - ment in the Cru - ci - fied? Are you
blood of the Lamb? Will your soul be read - y for the man - sions bright, And be
blood of the Lamb; There's a foun - tain flow - ing for the soul un - clean, O be

Chorus

washed in the blood of the Lamb? Are you washed in the blood,
Are you washed in the blood,

In the soul-cleans-ing blood of the Lamb? Are your gar - ments spot-less?
of the Lamb?

Are they white as snow? Are you washed in the blood of the Lamb?

Words And Music by E. A. Hoffman

PDHymns.com

287

A spiritual voyage into the pages of the Bible

Wonderful Words of Life

1. Sing them o - ver a - gain to me, Won - der - ful words of Life;
2. Christ, the bless - ed One, gives to all, Won - der - ful words of Life;
3. Sweet - ly ech - o the gos - pel call, Won - der - ful words of Life;

Let me more of their beau - ty see, Won - der - ful words of Life.
Sin - ner, list to the lov - ing call, Won - der - ful words of Life.
Of - fer par - don and peace to all, Won - der - ful words of Life.

Words of life and beau - ty, Teach me faith and du - ty;
All so free - ly giv - en, Woo - ing us to heav - en;
Je - sus, on - ly Sav - ior, Sanc - ti - fy for - ev - er;

Chorus

Beau - ti - ful words, won - der - ful words, Won - der - ful words of Life;

Beau - ti - ful words, won - der - ful words, Won - der - ful words of Life.

Words and Music: Phillip P. Bliss

Rescue The Perishing

1. Res - cue the per - ish - ing, Care for the dy - ing, Snatch them in pit - y from
2. Down in the hu - man heart, Crushed by the tempt - er, Feel - ings lie bur - ied that
3. Res - cue the per - ish - ing, Du - ty de - mands it; Strength for thy la - bor the

sin and the grave; Weep o'er the err - ing one, Lift up the fall - en,
grace can re - store; Touched by a lov - ing hand, Wak - ened by kind - ness,
Lord will pro - vide; Back to the nar - row way Pa - tient - ly win them;

Chorus

Tell them of Je - sus, the Might - y to save.
Chords that were bro - ken will vi - brate once more. Res - cue the per - ish - ing,
Tell the poor wan - d'rer a Sav - ior has died.

Care for the dy - ing; Je - sus is mer - ci - ful, Je - sus will save.

Words: Fanny J. Crosby
Music: William H. Doane

A spiritual voyage into the pages of the Bible

Be Still My Soul

Words by Katharina von Schlegel, Tr. by Jane L. Borthwick
Music by Jean Sibelius

Guide Me O Thou Great Jehovah

Words by William Williams
Music by John Hughes

PDHymns.com

The Church's One Foundation

Words by Samuel J. Stone
Music by M. Haydn

A spiritual voyage into the pages of the Bible

Sitting At The Feet Of Jesus

1. Sit - ting at the feet of Je - sus, Watch - ing, wait - ing ev - 'ry day; Trust-ing
2. List - 'ning at the feet of Je - sus, His com - mand to go or stay; Trust-ing
3. Seek - ing still the feet of Je - sus, I would seek no oth - er place; For 'tis
4. When the toils of life are o - ver, When my race on earth is run; May the

in His grace and pow - er, Safe to keep me all the way.
al - ways in His wis-dom, Safe to guide when I o - bey.
there I claim the prom - ise Of the full - ness of His grace.
eve - ning shad-ows gath'r-ing Find me there when day is done.

Chorus *FINE*

Sit-ting at the feet of

D.S.– Drive the shad - ows from my way.

D.S. al FINE

Je - sus, Where I love to kneel and pray, Til His good-ness and His glo - ry,

WORDS BY K. C. MINTER
MUSIC BY J. W. DAVIS

A spiritual voyage into the pages of the Bible

Come, Thou Almighty King

1. Come, Thou al - might - y King, Help us Thy name to sing,
2. Come, Thou in - car - nate Word, Gird on Thy might - y sword,
3. O Lord, our God, to Thee The high - est prais - es be,

Help us to praise! Fa - ther all glo - ri - ous, O'er all vic -
Our prayer at - tend! Come, and Thy peo - ple bless, And give Thy
Hence, ev - er - more; Thy sov - 'reign maj - es - ty May we in

to - ri - ous, Come and reign o - ver us, An - cient of Days!
word suc - cess: Spir - it of ho - li - ness, On us de - scend!
glo - ry see, And to e - ter - ni - ty Love and a - dore!

Words by Charles Wesley
Music by Felice de Giardini

A spiritual voyage into the pages of the Bible

Hallelujah What A Saviour

1. "Man of Sor-rows," what a name For the Son of God, Who came
2. Bear-ing shame and scoff-ing rude, In my place con-demned He stood,
3. Guilt-y vile and help-less we; Spot-less Lamb of God was He;
4. Lift-ed up was He to die, "It is fin-ished," was His cry;
5. When He comes, our glo-rious King, All His ran-somed home to bring,

Ru - ined sin - ners to re - claim! Hal - le - lu - jah! What a Sav - ior!
Sealed my par - don with His blood; Hal - le - lu - jah! What a Sav - ior!
"Full a - tone - ment!" can it be? Hal - le - lu - jah! What a Sav - ior!
Now in heav'n ex - alt - ed high, Hal - le - lu - jah! What a Sav - ior!
Then a - new this song we'll sing, Hal - le - lu - jah! What a Sav - ior!

Words and Music by Philip P. Bliss

A spiritual voyage into the pages of the Bible

Amazing Grace

Words by John Newton
Music by Early American Melody

Chapter 8
A Collection of Recipes

Paul's BBQ Sweet Potato & Corn

Ingredients:

- Some porc chops or steaks, whatever is on special that day!
- Corn in husks
- Sweet potato, sliced and drizzled with olive oil, no not Popeye's girlfriend, but the stuff squeezed out of olives by virgins don't you know!

Preparation:

- Put stuff on BBQ and cook till done!

Mary's Little Lamb With Bitter Herbs

Ingredients:

- One little lamb, snow white fleece optional
- Some hearty vegetables and bitter herbs
- Onions and garlic
- Greek olive oil
- One tall amaretto sour

Preparation:

- Lament in sackcloth and ashes for one week!
- Get lamb from Murray's on Van Horne avenue
- Roast lamb over an open pit in backyard

When Passover comes around, mostly before that Pagan holiday of Easter, it is important to remember what the lamb represents.

It represents Christ Jesus, the Lamb of God who was sacrificed in your place.

It also teaches that not 1 bone in Christ's body was broken during his Final day on Earth as the Lamb of God.

> Joh_19:36 For these things were done, that the scripture should be fulfilled, A bone of him shall not be broken.

Jackie's New Jersey Style Wings

Ingredients:

- 3 packs of chicken wings
- Seasoning salt and lemon pepper
- Garlic and onion powder
- Ginger
- Eggwash
- All-purpose flour, baking powder, corn starch

Preparation:

- Mix em up and fry in hot oil. Mmm mmm good!

Richard's Garden Pot Roast

Ingredients:

- Fresh garden vegetables
- Big chunk of browned red meat
- Freshly picked garden herbs
- Beef or vegetable broth with red wine

Preparation:

- Put everything in the crock pot and cook 4-6 hours.

Birthright Soup

Also known as lentil soup. Simple to make and an excellent source for Biblical teaching.

Bread

The Bible teaches that there are two types of bread!

The leavened, and the non leavened.

Some churches practise "The breaking of bread" that's nice and all, but do it right or don't do it at all!

If you are to "break bread" then use unleavened bread, a Matzo, else you are just ripping the Bulka, and missed the whole point of what the bread represents.

Vegan Food

Something for Vegans like Adam and Eve and all those that lived before Noah's flood.

A salad.

The All You Can Eat

After Noah's flood, God commanded Noah and his family to eat anything that moveth!

So EAT it all!

All is Kosher! The only forbidden thing commanded was and still is the commandment to not eat the blood of animals.

The Jewish Menu

Read the menu of authorized Kosher foods listed in Moses' 5 books, and Yes Virginia, locusts are on their menu!

But as a Christian you are not bound by their laws. If you start to keep their food laws, then you are obligated to keep all their laws. There is no pick and choose what's good for you.

Foods Sacrificed To Idols

It might look cute, tasty, and fun for the kids to eat, but..

Act 15:29 That ye abstain from meats offered to idols, and from blood, and from things strangled, and from fornication: from which if ye keep yourselves, ye shall do well. Fare ye well.

Jer. 7:18 The children gather wood, and the fathers kindle the fire, and the women knead *their* dough, to make cakes to the queen of heaven, and to pour out drink offerings unto other gods, that they may provoke me to anger.

One little bite is all it takes to seal your doom in the lake of fire! Leave the eggs and bunnies out of it, please.

Thank you.

The management.

A spiritual voyage into the pages of the Bible

Use this space for notes

Chapter 9
Lessons on prayer!

Below is Jesus's teaching on prayer, looks simple enough right?

> Luk 11:1   And it came to pass, that, as he was praying in a certain place, when he ceased, one of his disciples said unto him, Lord, teach us to pray, as John also taught his disciples.

> Luk 11:2   **And he said unto them,** When ye pray, say, Our Father which art in heaven, Hallowed be thy name. Thy kingdom come. Thy will be done, as in heaven, so in earth.

> Luk 11:3 Give us day by day our daily bread.

Luk 11:4 And forgive us our sins; for we also forgive every one that is indebted to us. And lead us not into temptation; but deliver us from evil.

Now let's see what it all means!

1)   How to begin;

When ye pray say!

That's it, no candles, no images, no rosary beads or crosses, no holy water, no incense, no schlepping yourself to church, just talk to God from wherever you are!

2)   Who to address;

Our Father! **NOT Jesus!**

3)   Whose name to revere;

Hallowed be thy name. God's name, Jesus always referred to God as "Father" "Heavenly Father".

As a **Born Again Christian** you are adopted into God's family! So you now have the privilege of calling God "Father", and thus Jesus becomes your brother!

4) Whose Kingdom are we to look for;

NOT the Kingdom of Heaven, but the Kingdom of God.

5) Whose will to obey;

Thy will be done. As in heaven, so in earth. God's will, NOT Jesus'.

6) What to ask for;

Give us day by day our daily bread. **Relying on God's provision and not self. You may also ask for whatsoever you want here!**

7) How to keep a clear channel to God;

And forgive us our sins. Remember you are a sinner like your father and mother before you. It won't kill you if you ask for forgiveness every day!

8) How to live with fellowmen;

For we also forgive every one that is indebted to us. You want to be forgiven, so then forgive those that offended you!

9)   How to live free from sin;

And lead us not into temptation; but deliver us from evil.

Rom 6:13   Neither yield ye your members *as* instruments of unrighteousness unto sin: but yield yourselves unto God, as those that are alive from the dead, and your members *as* instruments of righteousness unto God.

Rom 6:14   For sin shall not have dominion over you: for ye are not under the law, but under grace.

Rom 6:15   What then? shall we sin, because we are not under the law, but under grace? God forbid.

Rom 6:16   Know ye not, that to whom ye yield yourselves servants to obey, his servants ye are to whom ye obey; whether of sin unto death, or of obedience unto righteousness?

Rom 6:17   But God be thanked, that ye were the servants of sin, but ye have obeyed from the heart that form of doctrine which was delivered you.

Rom 6:18   Being then made free from sin, ye became the servants of righteousness.

Rom 6:19 I speak after the manner of men because of the infirmity of your flesh: for as ye have yielded your members servants to uncleanness and to iniquity unto iniquity; even so now yield your members servants to righteousness unto holiness.

Rom 6:20 For when ye were the servants of sin, ye were free from righteousness.

Rom 6:21 What fruit had ye then in those things whereof ye are now ashamed? for the end of those things *is* death.

Rom 6:22 But now being made free from sin, and become servants to God, ye have your fruit unto holiness, and the end everlasting life.

Rom 6:23 For the wages of sin *is* death; but the gift of God *is* eternal life through Jesus Christ our Lord.

Rom 8:12 Therefore, brethren, we are debtors, not to the flesh, to live after the flesh.

Rom 8:13 For if ye live after the flesh, ye shall die: but if ye through the Spirit do mortify the deeds of the body, ye shall live.

Quick tips on prayer!

1. Do not be like the hypocrites (The Jews) <u>read</u> <u>for</u> <u>yourself</u> what Jesus thought of their prayers.

2. God is a Person, so talk to God the Father like you talk to your friend!
   Humble yourself, and stop trying to impress God the Father with your knowledge of big fancy words in the English vocabulary.

3. Ask in faith, or don't ask at all!

4. Glorify God even before your prayer is answered, this shows your faith!

5. Use your power of attorney in Prayer to God the Father, always ASK in Jesus' name!

If you need lessons on Prayer 101 then contact us, and we will teach you the simplicity of getting answers from the Gods.

Note: Do not wait until your prayer is answered to praise God, praising God shows your faith!

Remember what the definition of faith is!

Heb 11:1 Now faith is the substance of things hoped for, the evidence of things not seen.

FREE GIFT OF ETERNAL LIFE
How To Become a Born-Again Christian in 3 Easy Steps

Step 1

The number one thing to do is **ADMIT** you are a sinner and worthy of spending eternity in Hell. If you can do that then you are halfway "Born Again."

Step 2

The second thing to do is to **PERSONALLY ACCEPT** Jesus Christ as your Lord and Savior.

> John 3:16 For God so loved the world, that he gave his only begotten Son, that whosoever believeth in him should not perish, but have everlasting life.

Step 3

The third and final step is to simply **BELIEVE AND HAVE FAITH** that God the Father has forgiven you, and that you have been adopted into the Holy Family.

> Hebrews 11:1 Now faith is the substance of things hoped for, the evidence of things not seen.

> Hebrews 11:2 For by it the elders obtained a good report.

That's it, you are done!

You are now a new creature, no need for any outward show, the change is a spiritual one, not a physical one!

Now if you have never read the Bible, that is fine, but it would be wise to start reading and obeying the truth as it is revealed to you in the Bible.

As a Christian start with the New Testament, and do not try to read the Bible as if it were some magical book with hidden meanings. Just read it as a child would, simply believing everything you read.

It is the simplest book to understand, and do not be like the Jewish people who say the average person cannot understand it and has to study the Talmud. For they are blind and cannot see the simplicity of the Word of God, for the main reason is that THEY DO NOT BELIEVE in Jesus the Christ (Messiah).

All can be saved with the Gospel. Hitler did not have to go to Hell if he followed the 3 simple steps above.

If you're stuck and not sure what to do, simply allow the Holy Spirit to guide you to the truth! Do not resist him!

Sin is sin, and it only takes 1 sin to seal your doom in the lake of fire. All are forgivable, but not all accept the FREE gift of God. Please do not harden your heart. Get saved right now, this moment, for tomorrow is not guaranteed.

A spiritual voyage into the pages of the Bible

Use this space for notes

How to reach us

http://tngchristians.ca

tngchristians@gmail.com

facebook.com/tngchristians

@TNGChristians

1-800-847-7820
(Toll Free in Canada and USA)